When Your Gay or Lesbian Child Marries

When Your Gay or Lesbian Child Marries

A Guide for Parents

Deborah M. Merrill

ROWMAN & LITTLEFIELD
Lanham • Boulder • New York • London

Published by Rowman & Littlefield
A wholly owned subsidiary of The Rowman & Littlefield Publishing Group, Inc.
4501 Forbes Boulevard, Suite 200, Lanham, Maryland 20706
www.rowman.com

Unit A, Whitacre Mews, 26-34 Stannary Street, London SE11 4AB

British Library Cataloguing in Publication Information Available

Library of Congress Cataloging-in-Publication Data

Merrill, Deborah M., 1962– author.
When your gay or lesbian child marries : a guide for parents / Deborah M. Merrill.
  pages cm
Includes bibliographical references and index.
ISBN 978-1-4422-5418-3 (cloth : alk. paper) — ISBN 978-1-4422-5419-0 (electronic)
1. Parents of gays—Family relationships. 2. Same-sex marriage. I. Title.
HQ759.9145.M47 2016
306.84'8—dc23   2015024613

∞™ The paper used in this publication meets the minimum requirements of American National Standard for Information Sciences—Permanence of Paper for Printed Library Materials, ANSI/NISO Z39.48-1992.

Printed in the United States of America

*This book is dedicated with admiration to my brother,
Larry Napoleone, who courageously battled ALS, and to my
sister-in-law, Gail Napoleone, who lovingly cared for him*

Contents

Acknowledgments

This book would not have been possible if not for the generosity of the men and women who volunteered to be interviewed. I am beholden to them for their assistance and honesty in sharing their life stories. I am also grateful to Denise Darrigrand for her help in identifying prospective respondents. Denise always gives well above what anyone could possibly hope for, and her assistance to me was no exception.

I am indebted to the sociology department at Clark University for the sheer joy in going to work each day. This includes Sarah Barry, Parminder Bhachu, Melissa Butler, Patty Ewick, Bruce London, Debi Osnowitz, Bob Ross, Shelly Tenenbaum, and Rosalie Torres-Stone. We have had an amazing twenty-three years together. Thanks also to associate provost and dean of research Nancy Budwig, who has always encouraged my research. I am also grateful to Clark University for a faculty development grant to compensate respondents for their participation in this study.

Special thanks to my family for their love and support, particularly to my mom, Nancy Merrill, and to her partner, Bob Thiers. I extend my gratitude as well to my extended family, one and all, and to my dearest friend, Kristen Williams, and her family for their unconditional love. Thank you to Andrea Figueroa and Ellen Chevalier, who keep me physically fit despite sitting at my desk all day, and to Jane Daigneault, Jackie Geoghegan, Nina Kushner, Doug and Pat Little, Frank and Barbara Piscitelli, Laurie Porter, Amy Richter, Valerie Sperling, and Mark and Susan Turnbull for their years of friendship. Many thanks to the members of the UUCWorcester for their friendship and to Reverend Aaron Payson for his inspiration and example. Finally, a special thank you to Julie Zork, LMFT, for everything, and to my husband, Ken Basye, who is everything.

Chapter 1

Introduction

The purpose of this book is to introduce to the parents of gay and lesbian adult children all of the various contours of same-sex marriage, such as its unique characteristics, similarities to heterosexual marriage, and the wide range of experiences of its members. The second purpose is to describe to parents how their relationships with their adult children will change over the course of their children's lives, particularly at the points when the child discloses his or her sexual orientation and after the adult child's marriage. It is meant to be a primer for parents and other family members as they transition to becoming the mothers and fathers of a gay or lesbian child and at other critical junctions in their child's life. The book begins with an overview of what is known about parent and adult child ties as well as information on the nature of same-sex marriage in America today.

BACKGROUND ON PARENT–ADULT CHILD RELATIONSHIPS

Relationships between parents and their adult children are a central component of family life and social ties, with the mother-and-daughter relationship being the closest of the four possible dyads.[1] They are an important source of psychological well-being throughout the life course for both parents and adult children.[2] The quality of the relationship runs the gamut from alienated to tight knit, although most are generally positive with relative geographic nearness, frequent contact, and emotional closeness.[3] Intergenerational relationships, such as the parent-child bond, however, are complex and can rarely be characterized along one dimension. In addition to a high degree of affection, conflict

1

is often present as well. This "ambivalence" is greater the closer the family relationship.[4] That is, the nearer that one is to a family member (such as an immediate family member versus an extended family member), the greater the likelihood of feeling disappointed or concerned about the person's life choices and their implications for one's self. Close family members may feel freer to voice those concerns, also leading to conflict. Ambivalence is often manifested during transitions, or life-changing events, experienced by either adult children or their parents.[5] This suggests that the adult child's marriage may be a time in which difficulties will arise in the relationship.

In addition to affection, obligation, and the exchange of resources, such as the sharing of money, are the other two main cornerstones of intergenerational relationships. In fact, obligations to one's own parents and children rank the highest of all personal relationships.[6] This includes the obligation to provide emotional support, which may be difficult when one is concerned about the life path that a parent or child is taking and its implications for that person's well-being. A child may be concerned that his or her parent is marrying someone who does not love them and is instead looking for financial gain. The parents' concern may be that their child is marrying a partner too quickly, for the "wrong" reasons, or who is ill suited to them. Parents worry that a child's marriage may prevent them from being financially secure, having children, advancing in their career, or otherwise being happy. Obligation also includes the provision of financial and caregiving assistance to the generations above and below oneself. For that reason, each generation is particularly aware of, or may even be critical of, the steps taken by the other and feels greater vested interest in a parent or child's circumstances than the circumstances of extended family members. Parents and adult children share financial resources, emotional support, and companionship, as well as practical assistance, such as a grandparent babysitting for grandchildren. What is exchanged though depends upon the direction of the flow of resources. The exchange of financial aid and services tends to go from parents to adult children only.[7] Emotional support is more common than financial assistance, and it usually goes in both directions. There is significant disagreement among researchers, however, on the potential impact of a daughter's divorce on the provision of financial assistance.[8] In contrast, adult children provide their parents with companionship, affection, and finally caregiving, with African Americans and Asian Americans being even more likely to endorse norms of filial obligation than white Caucasians.[9]

Intergenerational relationships differ significantly though by the various combinations of male versus female members of the family. Mothers and daughters tend to be closer to other family members than do fathers and sons. In addition, the wife's parents are likely to provide and receive more assistance than the husband's parents following a child's marriage.[10] While both men and women report feeling closer to their own parents than to their in-laws, the difference is greater for women than for men.[11] In addition, although men may feel greater affection for their own parents, they have more contact with their in-laws than do women.[12] How these gender differences play out in same-sex marriages, however, is currently unknown.

Parent–adult child relationships are also affected by the life course and the events that occur within it. For example, mothers experience ambivalence when children do not meet expected life-course markers, such as becoming financially independent, marrying, and having children.[13] Likewise, relationships between parents and adult children tend to worsen when parents start to need help, thus redirecting the earlier flow of assistance from parent to child.[14] Parent-child relationships are also affected by the marriage of either the child or a parent. For example, remarried parents provide less support to their adult children than continuously married parents.[15] A remarriage can also affect the likelihood of a child inheriting later on in life, thus affecting the relationship with one's parent as well as stepparent.[16] An adult child's marriage also impacts the relationship. Both married men and women have less intense intergenerational ties than never-married and divorced individuals.[17] According to those who study this phenomenon, marriage is a "greedy institution" that takes time away from relationships with other family members and the community. Daughters tend to remain close to their parents following marriage, while sons get pulled into their wives' families and have lessened contact with their own parents.[18] This results from an expectation in our society that daughters will *always* remain close to their parents, while sons have greater leeway to pull back from the relationship following marriage.

The quality of intergenerational relationships and the factors that affect that quality are important for a number of reasons. Parent–adult child bonds are a key source of feeling whole or complete in the world for both parents and their adult children and significantly affect psychological functioning. Yet, the negative aspects of intergenerational relationships, such as conflict and estrangement, are more strongly associated with psychological distress than the positive aspects are associated with psychological well-being.[19] Thus, problems in the relationship that result from same-sex marriages could cause significant psychological distress, such as depression or anxiety, for both adult children and their parents. We already know that gay and lesbian cohabiting couples perceive less support from families than heterosexual couples.[20] Lack of support from key family members like parents has a significant impact on same-sex relationships though. For example, social support from any chosen family member is important for the quality of the couple's relationship.[21] In addition, alienated or conflicted relationships also decrease the likelihood of children providing care for their elderly parents. With the aging of the baby boomers and the need for filial care for widowed parents, estranged and conflicted parent-child relationships pose a significant threat to an aging society and aging families. Finally, conflict between parents and adult children or children-in-law also undermines the adult child's marriage.[22] In an era in which divorce rates remain high and there is concern that marriage is only one of a number of equivalent adult living arrangements, understanding and decreasing stressors on marriage are a benefit to everyone.

SAME-SEX MARRIAGE

Intergenerational relationships of all types are affected by not only the course or trajectory of one's life and when events occur, such as when a woman has her children, but the time period as well. Today young adult child and parent relationships are impacted by the growing availability and acceptance of same-sex marriage. In May 2004, Massachusetts became the first state to legalize same-sex marriage. Nine years later, over seventy-one thousand same-sex marriages had been granted in the nine states of California, Connecticut, Iowa, Maine, Massachusetts, New Hampshire, New York, Vermont, and Washington.[23] By October 2014, marriage was legal in thirty states with challenges pending in the other twenty states.[24] However, in June 2015, the U.S. Supreme Court overruled the rights of these states to deny marriage and made it possible for same-sex couples in all states to marry. Sixteen countries also grant same-sex marriage. These countries include Canada, Brazil, Argentina, Uruguay, South Africa, New Zealand, and much of Western Europe. More than half, 60 percent, of Americans say that homosexuality should be accepted by society, up from 49 percent in 2007.[25] In 2009, estimates suggested that there were approximately 581,300 same-sex couples in the United States, a likely underestimate, and that the growth in same-sex couples was outpacing population growth.[26]

Not all couples whose relationships can be legally recognized choose to seek that legal status though. In 2008, 40 percent of same-sex couples who were living in states that legally recognized their relationships were in such a union. Nearly one-quarter, or 21 percent, of marriages in those states that year were for same-sex couples.[27] However, the fact that the percentages are as high as they are suggests the importance of marriage, typically seen as a traditional institution, to individuals in a gay or lesbian relationship.

The right to marry has been a contentious issue in all states and a hard-won victory for proponents of gay rights. Following Massachusetts' passage in 2004, many states added amendments to their state constitutions explicitly banning same-sex marriage. Earlier the federal government attempted to limit couples' rights to marry and to slow pending state legislation with the Defense of Marriage Act passed in September 1996. DOMA, which allowed states to refuse to recognize marriages performed in another state and which barred married couples from receiving federal benefits, however, was found unconstitutional in 2013.

Same-sex couples choose to marry for reasons that are very similar to heterosexual couples. This includes a desire to express a commitment to the relationship and an intention to stay together in front of friends and family. Such an expression of this commitment is believed to cement the bond at a meaningful time in the relationship. For couples that have or intend to have children, their marriage is believed to ensure the children's well-being by providing an optimal place to raise children and guaranteeing the rights of both parents. Heterosexual and homosexual couples also recognize the importance of state and federal legal benefits from marriage, including the right to inherit from a deceased spouse and significant tax breaks for the couple. In addition, for some, the decision to marry is a political statement about gay and lesbian rights and an opportunity to challenge traditional marriage and create greater gender equity. American gay men and lesbians (as well as those from the Netherlands, where same-sex marriage has been legal since 2001) are strikingly similar to American heterosexual men and women in statements about marriage and childbearing as well. For example, American heterosexuals view same-sex marriage as "true" marriage and treat married same-sex couples similarly to heterosexual ones. Some gay, lesbian, and heterosexual couples have even chosen not to marry as a type of protest, since marriage was not available to everyone over eighteen years of age in the United States until recently.[28]

Not all homosexual couples are equally likely to marry. Lesbian couples are more likely to enter into marriage than gay male couples. In fact, lesbian couples prefer marriage to other adult living arrangements regardless of its availability.[29] In addition, lower levels of education and income increase the likelihood of a same-sex couple marrying.[30] These individuals may wish to marry for the financial benefits. However, same-sex partners earn less than heterosexual married partners.[31]

Not surprisingly, marital status affects the likelihood of becoming a parent in the gay and lesbian community. Married same-sex couples are twice as likely to have children as unmarried same-sex couples. Nearly one-third (31 percent) of married couples have children in comparison to 17 percent of unmarried couples. Whether couples with children are more likely to want to marry or vice versa, however, is unclear. The fact that nearly one-third of married couples have offspring though suggests the importance of children to gay and lesbian couples that intend to stay together.[32] This implies that homosexual couples, in at least some regards, are seeking a family life that is similar to heterosexual marriage.

The likelihood of a married homosexual couple staying together is, as yet, unclear. We do know that heterosexual couples have a lower rate of divorce and separation than gay and lesbian couples over a five-year period (7 percent versus 14 percent and 16 percent respectively).[33] This may be due to the fact that homosexual couples receive less support from friends and family or experience more stressors than heterosexual couples.[34] In fact, half of interracial same-sex couples say that their sexual orientation is more stressful than being in an interracial marriage.[35] Lesbians are more likely to dissolve their relationships than gay men though, likely due to their heightened sensitivity to the quality of the relationship.[36]

Other researchers have found that the breakup rate for same-sex married couples is similar to heterosexual married couples once you control for the lower rate of marriages among same-sex couples. Same-sex couples who have a marriage-like commitment have relationships as equally stable as heterosexual married couples. According to this same research, lesbian couples and gay male couples have similar levels of couple stability. Lesbians are more likely to be married or coresident in comparison to gay couples though.[37]

Gay and lesbian couples are similar to heterosexuals in other aspects as well. In half of the dimensions of relationship quality, gays and lesbians cohabiting do not differ from married heterosexuals. Where there is a difference, 78 percent of the comparisons show gays and lesbians functioning *better* than heterosexual couples. This suggests that the processes that affect how well a heterosexual relationship functions can be generalized to gay and lesbian couples as well.[38] In other words, gay and lesbian couples are not all that different from heterosexual couples.

In some ways though, gay and lesbian couples are in fact unlike heterosexual couples. In particular, gay and lesbian couples are more likely to distribute household labor equally, relative to heterosexual couples.[39] For example, in the Netherlands, same-sex married couples do not assign breadwinner versus homemaker roles to spouses. All of the spouses in the study conducted in the Netherlands were employed outside of the home, if only part time.[40] Same-sex parents tend to be both involved in parenting and "hands on" with their children.[41] The ability of the family to function successfully is also higher and conflict is lower for gay and lesbian households relative to heterosexual ones.[42] Lesbian couples perceive higher levels of equality in their relationship and express more positive perceptions of their partners than heterosexuals.[43] Gay and lesbian relationships also reflect more compatibility and intimacy than do heterosexual unions. However, some research shows that most gay couples are not monogamous (that is, they have more than one sexual relationship), even after marriage.[44] Thus, at least some same-sex couples reject the traditional aspects of marriage. The question remains as to whether they will also reject the traditional aspects of parent–adult child relationships and in-law dynamics following marriage.

Other studies have found that gay men's long-lasting relationships are similar to heterosexual marriages and are not overly sexualized. They focus on cozy togetherness, companionship, and partnership. Sex alone does not play a predominant role in the lives of long-term gay couples, as many in society believe. Instead, there is a propensity for gay men to conform to existing, mostly heterosexual, norms. Overall, the research suggests that the gay population is not one single community. Instead, there is great heterogeneity across the gay experience.[45]

RESEARCH QUESTIONS TO BE ADDRESSED IN THIS BOOK

Events that occur across a person's life course, such as marriage, have a significant impact on other social ties, such as relationships with one's parents. The assumption of a new role, like becoming a spouse, creates other role changes across the entirety of one's life course. Differences in attitudes of what is acceptable or not across generations, often referred to as a "generation gap," may place significant barriers on the ability of the parent and child to agree on the appropriateness of either one taking on a new role, such as becoming a same-sex partner. There are also significant gender differences in how people experience life-course events. An earlier study of heterosexual marriages showed that daughters continue to stay close to their parents following their marriages while sons often pull away.[46] This was due, in part, to the overall expectation that daughters will stay connected to their parents. In contrast, sons sometimes spend less time with their parents because of an increased focus on their work and the provider role, despite changes from the gender "revolution" since the 1960s. In addition, a son's relationship with his parents is somewhat mediated by his wife, who pulls him into *her* family. Mothers say that they are less "at home" in their married son's house than their married daughter's house and that their sons spend less time with them following marriage than do their daughters.

The purpose of this book is to examine whether same-sex marriage has similar or different effects on parent–adult child relationships in comparison to heterosexual marriage and the causes of those similarities and differences. It is also a primer for parents on what same-sex marriage is like. Supporters of same-sex marriage posit that the nontraditional aspects of gay and lesbian unions will create changes in the meaning of marriage.[47] The premise of this book is that these nontraditional aspects of same-sex marriage will also affect the extended family and family relationships. The fact that same-sex marriage is a new phenomenon will provide a clean slate to rewrite the expectations of family dynamics and relationships, such as the differences that occur when a son versus a daughter marries.

Additional factors related to homosexuality or being the parent of a gay or lesbian child will also impact parent–adult child relationships. Gay and lesbians report receiving less parental support before marriage than heterosexuals.[48] How will this then affect parent–adult child relationships? Parents of homosexual adults also tend to worry more about them.[49] Concerns that gay and lesbian children will not attain the joys of a "normal" life, such as having children, will also cause greater negative emotions for parents. Likewise, children may feel more ambivalence or anger if their parents see them as different from their heterosexual siblings or if their parents do not fully accept their spouses. Parent-and-child relationships may also be affected by their history, such as a homosexual child's earlier problems with school or the parent's own difficulty in accepting their child's first manifestations of their gay/lesbian identity. In addition, parent-child relationships may be impacted by parents' fears of what others will think as a child's marriage is made public.

Family life occurs within an overall system that is affected by both external, or environmental, factors and internal factors, such as the relative beliefs of family members. "Coming out" to one's family is a pivotal event that changes the way that all members of the family interrelate.[50] However, the family system will also affect the experience of being gay/lesbian. How any one family member reacts to someone "coming out" or marrying someone of the same sex will depend upon their gender, education, income, age, and the way that other family members respond. Still, everyone in the family holds his or her own unique perspective, and new family members introduced into the system or new experiences may change a member's viewpoint on a topic. As such, there are often unexpected and unanticipated turns in people's relationships and attitudes.[51] Earlier research shows that families that are high in both closeness and ability to adapt to new circumstances report more contact with GLBT (gay, lesbian, bisexual, or transsexual) family members.[52] Will that then translate into better relationships, and what about other families with lower levels of closeness or adaptability? Likewise, if the family is a whole system where what happens with one member affects everyone else, how will extended family members respond to a grandchild's or sibling's same-sex marriage? How will the responses of the broader family affect the parents' response to their child's sexual orientation? Will the fact that grandchildren will be adopted, versus being biological grandchildren, affect how grandparents connect to their gay/lesbian children and subsequent grandchildren? Mothers and fathers may also respond differently to their child's initial "coming out" as well as subsequent dating and marriage.

This book will also address whether or not gay and lesbian couples will be able to avoid some of the negative outcomes of heterosexual marriage, particularly the conflict with in-laws that sometimes occurs.[53] It is expected that the nontraditional relationships of gays and lesbians will lead to improved relationships with in-laws and that in-law conflict instead arises from the way that family relationships differ for sons versus daughters and fathers versus mothers. In-law conflict can be avoided if a *son-in-law* is not seen as competition for a son's attention and time the way that a daughter-in-law is. In contrast, parents can be close to their daughters' same-sex partners because of the presumed closeness of female family members in general. Women will be more likely to share time with one another's parents because of the more egalitarian, or equal, nature of their relationships relative to heterosexual couples. Likewise, there will be less conflict with a son's husband because of the presumed independence of men in the family. Sons will freely visit their families without expectations of bringing their spouses along. Earlier researchers have contended that heterosexual marriage is a "greedy institution."[54] I will argue here, however, that same-sex marriages are less greedy of the individuals that inhabit them. Thus, the nontraditional nature of the marriage and the new combinations of gender dynamics will change family relationships. It is the continued reinforcement of differences for men versus women in heterosexual marriage that creates our current expectations of marriage and its effects on other family relationships.[55] Without that gender differentiation though, how will marriage change, including the impact on parent-child and in-law relationships?

Overall, this book will look at how people with different sexual orientations and their families "do family" or fulfill the roles and perform the practices of family.[56] Same-sex marriage can change the relationships between parents and adult children because they do not have the constraints of conventional heterosexual marriage.

This book will also look at whether or not same-sex marriage will transform what we mean by marriage in society. Will same-sex marriage just replicate the roles and expectations of heterosexual family patterns and relationships? Alternatively, will same-sex marriage make homosexuality an equal and publicly known alternative to heterosexuality? Some individuals argue that same-sex marriage does change the institution of marriage but in a negative direction. They claim that it displaces formerly core public understandings of marriage.[57] That is, by redefining what we mean by marriage, we are undermining it. In the Netherlands, same-sex marriage does not significantly change people's perceptions of marriage, including the choice to marry and its purposes.[58] However, same-sex couples do not try to re-create the traditional roles of "husband" and "wife" but instead reject a division between breadwinner and homemaker roles. One could therefore expect them not to reproduce traditional roles of in-laws as well. Relatively little changed in the Netherlands in the larger cultural landscape of marriage once same-sex couples could marry. Marriage remained the preferred status for both heterosexuals and homosexuals. In the United States, however, there has been evidence that same-sex couples are more likely to distribute housework equally and to value equality more and that they tend to be more compatible and intimate and experience less conflict.[59] Likewise, the great diversity of homosexual experiences is likely to position it outside of the expectations of heterosexuality.[60] Thus, same-sex marriage may be more likely to change the institution of marriage in the United States than in the Netherlands. Finally, will the lack of institutional and parental support for same-sex marriage undermine the couple's relationship, relative to heterosexual couples?

Information from an earlier study of the impact of heterosexual marriage on parent-child relationships will be used for comparison to same-sex couples.[61] This information includes interviews with twenty-five mothers who have at least one married (heterosexual) child and one unmarried child as well as twenty-five heterosexual, married sons or daughters with at least one living parent. These heterosexuals and mothers of heterosexuals will then be compared to thirty individuals in same-sex marriages, including fifteen lesbians and fifteen gay men, all of whom have at least one living parent, and ten parents, including fathers, with at least one child in a same-sex marriage and one child in a heterosexual marriage. All of the interviews were conducted in Massachusetts where same-sex marriage has been legal for the longest period in the United States. This allowed for the opportunity to look at relatively long-term effects and allowed for the recruitment of a wide array of individuals. The data were collected between May 2012 and December 2013, or eight to nine years after the introduction of same-sex marriage. See the appendix for a more extensive discussion of the data collection and analysis. Please note that the respondents' words are presented verbatim without editing and without judgment. Also, respondents sometimes present ideas and experiences that reflect stereotypes that are not necessarily factual.

OUTLINE OF THE BOOK

Chapter 2 considers the experiences of families when their gay and lesbian children "come out of the closet" or make known their sexual orientation. It also examines how mothers and fathers redefine what it means to be the parent of a gay or lesbian child and how the family as a system changes following disclosure. Gender differences in the reactions of mothers versus fathers are analyzed.

Chapter 3 looks at the quality and nature of the relationship between parents and their gay or lesbian children, including when the children were young. It also examines the different perspectives of sons versus daughters and of fathers versus mothers. Factors that affect the quality of the relationship are discussed. Overall, conflict and disappointment regarding the child's sexual orientation cause gay and lesbian adult children and their parents to stipulate qualifications when describing even the most positive relationships. The unconditional love and obligation that define intergenerational relationships result in parents and children maintaining at least some contact even when there is discord in the relationship. Parental concerns suggest the continued presumption of heterosexuality in American society. However, the fact that younger parents are more likely to be accepting of their gay and lesbian children provides evidence of a generational shift toward greater support of homosexuality, but perhaps not as an equivalent alternative to heterosexuality.

Chapter 4 examines the effect of marriage on the relationship between parents and gay or lesbian adult children. Marriage worsens relationships between parents and *heterosexual* sons because sons step back from their family of orientation to focus on their own families. They also tend to get pulled into their wives' families since it is usually wives who schedule the couple's social calendar. Relationships between parents and their married gay sons are relatively better than relationships with heterosexual sons, as is the relationship between the parents and their gay/lesbian children-in-law. The reasons for this are discussed, including the implications of gender differences for husbands versus wives in heterosexual marriage and what happens when those expectations are lifted.

Chapter 5 considers the reasons that same-sex versus heterosexual couples choose to marry. Included are both political and nonpolitical reasons for marriage. The fact that so many couples continue to choose to marry is a particularly perplexing topic given the continued high divorce rate and range of alternative living arrangements for couples. The reasons for marrying given by homosexuals will help to shed light on their perceptions of marriage and their meanings and how they differ from heterosexuals. This chapter will also consider how same-sex versus heterosexual couples divide labor in the home. This allows us to discern whether and how same-sex marriage may be changing the nature of marriage, or not, in America.

Chapter 6 looks at parenting for same-sex couples. This includes a discussion of the process by which same-sex couples decide whether or not to have children, their options for acquiring a child, and the factors that they consider in their choices. It also examines how same-sex couples "do parenting" and how that differs from heterosexual parenting and any particular challenges that same-sex couples face as parents.

Chapter 7 examines the effect of sexual orientation on a couple's relationship with one another. In particular, it considers whether there are factors related to their homosexuality that bring the couple together or that drive a wedge between spouses. Likewise, it examines how the lack of gender differences and the "clean slate" that comes with new forms of marriage impact the couple and their marital bond.

Chapter 8 considers the reactions of the entire extended family to the couple's marriage and the factors that affect their relationship with their gay or lesbian family member. It considers the family as a system where the behavior of one family member affects all other members of the system and where emergent properties arise from the sum of the parts of the system. Also examined is the effect of the overall family culture on how it responds to one person's homosexuality and the nature of family connections.

Chapter 9 examines how same-sex couples "do family," that is, perform the functions of different family roles and how that differs from heterosexuals. This includes how couples share power and the division of labor, how lesbians parent, and how gay men and lesbians relate to parents and in-laws as well as to their extended families. This chapter also examines the advice that adult children in same-sex marriages give to other lesbians and gay men and the advice that parents provide to other parents of newly disclosed or newly married homosexuals.

Chapter 2

"Coming Out"

Relationships between parents and their gay or lesbian child are first affected when the parents learn of their child's homosexuality. This information is usually provided by the child himself or herself. "Coming out of the closet" or disclosing one's sexual orientation as being lesbian or gay is a pivotal event that forever changes the family as an entire system of interrelated individuals.[1] Coming out not only alters relationships between the lesbian or gay individual and family members but also has the potential to change relationships between the additional members of the family who will often react differently to the news. It can worsen preexisting tensions and conflicts and result in placing blame on one another. Disclosure can result in a generational divide or sever a marriage. Leading up to the disclosure is the son or daughter's decision to lead a double life and to deceive one's family or to risk rejection by sharing one's identity as gay or lesbian.[2]

To whom one discloses and when or how is a selective process. It is predicated on religion, geographic location, race/ethnicity, and the family member's assumed perspective on issues of gender equality and sexuality.[3] Children may come out first to the parent who is most likely to be accepting of the news, especially if they believe that their parents will not respond uniformly. They may want to tell each parent themselves, whether together or separately, or allow one parent to tell the other. Uppermost in the adult children's mind though is their perception of how they believe their parents will react, dependent upon a lifetime of interactions and acquired knowledge of their parents.

Family reactions to the news can run the gamut from total acceptance to hostility.[4] Responses may include total estrangement, silence/

denial, disappointment, tentative acknowledgement, or complete support.[5] The "transparent closet" or "family closet" refers to situations where a family member is told but refuses to acknowledge their child's sexual orientation.[6] The person remains in denial. Individuals who do come out of the closet know that once the information has been shared, they can no longer take for granted the unconditional love and acceptance that one expects of family.[7] It is seen as one of the few acceptable reasons for the estrangement of parent-and-child relationships.

Everyone in the family will hold his or her own unique perspective on the individual's homosexuality, depending on family role, age, gender and sexuality awareness, and unique life experiences, such as education. It is assumed that each family member will steadily become more accepting or not change at all. However, the process of change is more likely to be a nonlinear one. There may be regressions or pockets of homophobia as family members gradually begin the process of acceptance.[8] New information and experiences may also hasten this consent. Other family members though may become less accepting as the initial information sets in or as they encounter experiences that reinforce their own homophobia. Overall, even the most positive parent–adult child relationships are strained in the process of coming out.[9]

Parents must reenvision and redefine what it means to be a parent of a gay or lesbian child following the process of coming out.[10] This may include having new goals for their child, new fears or concerns, and a desire to protect their child from a homophobic society where there is significant unease around homosexuality. Parents know that they too will have to disclose their child's sexual orientation to others, and they too will be judged as the parent of a homosexual. They may even judge or blame themselves. Parents will also have to redefine their understanding of their child based on new information that may conflict with a lifetime of assumptions of their child and who he or she is. For some, it will be similar to having a "new" child in the family, one that they know only partially.

This chapter will focus on the early years in the parent–adult child relationship and the process of coming out. It will consider topics that have not previously been discussed such as differences in the reactions of mothers versus fathers and just how the family system changes as a result of a child announcing his or her homosexuality. It will examine what the parents' perceptions of their child's sexual orientation were before they came out and the process that they went through as they adjusted to the information. It is the first account of statements by both parents and adult children in the United States following the passage of the Massachusetts' same-sex marriage law and will help parents to understand all of the nuances of their child's journey as a gay man or lesbian.

THE YEARS PRIOR TO DISCLOSURE

Learning that a child is gay or a lesbian is often not a complete surprise. Parents perceived their children as somehow "different" during the years that they were growing up. Colleen explained,

> I knew that Dominic was gay when he was about three. He was very different from the other boys his age. . . . Dominic was more sensitive—more thoughtful. He would say, "Mommy, what did you do today?" when I picked him up from day care, and he would go over to a kid who was crying and put his arm around him. . . . [He] would tell me when someone had been sad at day care. Even back then, Dominic [who is a drag queen] would dress up in heels and dresses. He liked to play with dressup, but he also liked the boys more than the girls. He was attracted to them—in an odd way that I did not see with other boys.

Likewise, Sharon stated,

> Shannon wasn't a tomboy, but she wasn't feminine either. She just did not fit into any category. . . . I would try to put her in a dress for school pictures, and she just looked so awkward, like it didn't fit her. Her hair never grew out like a girl's does. She never had a girl's body, skinny or curvy. She was built like a fireplug, always. But like I said, it wasn't that she was a tomboy. She wasn't athletic or daring. . . . Later, she never had any interest in boys or dances or movie stars. She was just so different from her sister—and the other girls. Shannon had a few good friends, but she was always on the outside of things.

Thus, growing up has been difficult for these children because of their differences from other children. As a result, parents worried about their children when they were young and experienced more tribulations with them compared to their other children. Lisa explained,

> My son is a dancer. Others have always picked on him . . . since he was an adolescent. Even now, he has to change [out of] his dancer's shoes before he goes out into public or he risks someone assaulting him or harassing, even around here. When he was growing up, he was always bullied. I was constantly worried. I would go to school and talk to his teachers and the principal. I did not want to baby him, but I did not want to see him hurt either. . . . It was awful for both of us. He said once that it was a good thing that he did not come out in high school

because he would have been ridiculed. . . . He knew that he did not fit in like the other boys and it made him very self-conscious.

Some of the mothers described how hard it was for their husbands to accept their sons while they were growing up. Barb said,

> I think that we all realized that Ryan was gay when he was around 10 or 11. He was very effeminate. My husband would say "queer." He walked like, well, like a gay. [Barb was an older parent who espoused stereotypes of gay men that are generally discredited today.] His hair had to be just so, and his clothes too. He did not like sports. [Ryan] always wanted to go to the hair salon with me to watch the girls doing hair. . . . He painted his nails in secret, although I knew that he was doing it. . . . [This] was when my husband started leaving the house when Ryan was around. He did not want to say anything that he would regret, and I think that he does love Ryan, but he just could not be around him. He could not see him, like that. . . . Maybe he also hoped that Ryan would change. I don't know. . . . But Ryan knew why his dad was leaving. I think he felt that his father was rejecting him. . . . It was then that his problems started. [Ryan later became an alcoholic.]

Parents, especially fathers, have greater difficulty accepting gay sons than lesbian daughters when they are young. This is likely due to a lower acceptance in our society overall of effeminate men, who are still seen as weak and outside of the fringes of acceptable behavior. Lisa, for example, pointed out that although her son is physically fit and strong, people on the subway still make fun of him if he has on his dancing shoes or if he exhibits a more feminine demeanor. Connor has even learned how to present himself as, or to act, straight in order to avoid being bullied. In contrast, a woman who is exhibiting more male or androgynous behavior is more likely to be accepted, due to the greater value that we place on strength and masculinity in our society. In fact, the boundaries of what is female may be far more expansive in our society due in part to the women's liberation and feminist movements, while there have been no such movements for men and the constraints of being male. Likewise, gay sexual practices are still seen as more deviant in American society than lesbian practices.

Many of the adult children in the study did not realize that they were gay or lesbian until they met their partner or went to college, where it was more accepted versus in their own community. Siobhan, who went to an all-women's college, said that she might not have ever realized she was a lesbian if she had gone to a co-ed college, where lesbian relationships and opportunities to meet lesbians are less commonplace. Instead, she realized she was attracted to women during her first week of college, despite having never had an inkling of such beforehand. She said, "I had my first experience with a woman that first week in college. She became my first girlfriend. I have had several long term relationships [with women] since then, but I have never looked back [to being straight]."

Other homosexuals realize they are homosexual during their sexual awakenings. Ben explained,

Oh, I knew that I was gay at the beginning . . . well, maybe not at the very beginning. But, I remember when my dad showed me a book on how babies are born, and I had an erection when I saw the erect penis. . . . Of course, I did not know what being gay was then. But I was never attracted to girls, and I knew that being attracted to boys was not something others seemed to do. I did not go to dances, but I did go to the senior prom. I was supposedly by myself, but I really was meeting up with my lover there. Anyway, I heard the term *Homo* when I was in fourth grade and what it meant. It was then that I knew what I was, but I did not tell anyone until late high school.

Older gays and lesbians, many of whom became adults when homosexuality was still much more taboo than today, had physical relationships with the *opposite* sex well into adulthood. Charlotte and Natalia were even engaged to men following college. It was not until they were roommates in their late twenties that they realized they wanted to be more than just friends with one another. In contrast, several other older men and women had been in heterosexual marriages before coming out. All stated that they had not realized they were homosexual when they married the first time. Ed recognized he was gay when he was around twenty-five years of age and had been married for two years. Likewise, Nancy acknowledged after five or six years of marriage that she was more attracted to other women that she knew at work than she was to her husband. Melissa tried to deny her lesbian interests, which she discovered after her first child was born. It was not until her daughter was twelve years of age and she met the woman who would become her wife that she was willing to leave her husband and home and move in with her girlfriend along with her daughter.

Some of the sons experienced difficult relationships with their fathers or stepfathers early in life. Steve, for example, said that his stepfather was determined to "butch him up" while he was younger. Steve's stepfather would take him to the ballpark and drill him in running and hitting the ball. His stepdad would make him stay longer if he started to cry and would make fun of him when he missed the ball. Steve said that it was "bordering abuse" because he

was such a poor athlete. Steve remembered this occurring episodically whenever his stepfather grew frustrated with having a gay son. His stepdad also
forbade him from having boyfriends to their home or even being with them
on the street. To this day, Steve is not allowed to bring his spouse with him
when he visits his mother and stepfather.

More men than women often find it difficult to accept their sexuality when
they first discover it. This is likely due to the greater stigma that we attach
to being gay versus lesbian in our society. Younger men, however, were less
likely to reject being gay than were older men, suggesting there may be an
increased acceptance today. Bob, in his early seventies, shared the following:

> I have led a double life for many years . . . more years than I want to tell you.
> I was married and had a lover on the side. He was married too. We both had kids.
> It was okay though because we were both in the same boat. We knew that noth-
> ing was ever going to come of it [the relationship]. . . . Then I got a divorce. My
> wife said that I was not "attuned to her needs." Of course not. I loved someone
> else. She still does not know today. Neither do my kids. I am married to this
> wonderful man, but I cannot share it outside of our circle. I just can't [*looking
> as if he might cry*]. I don't want them to know.

Bob's children live in another part of the country, and he visits them alone.
Bob's colleagues are also not aware of his marriage.

"MOM AND DAD, THERE IS SOMETHING
YOU SHOULD KNOW"

Parents' reactions to their children disclosing their sexuality runs the gamut
from walking away from their child to being happy about the news. Siobhan
shared the following:

> I called my mother that first week that I was in college and told her that I was
> a lesbian. She was actually happy about it . . . and still is today. I think that she
> liked the fact that I was different, not traditional. . . . My parents never had any
> expectation of marriage for us, or of a wedding, grandchildren. . . . They just
> wanted us to have good jobs, so it was just fine with her. I left it to her to tell
> my father, and he had a harder time with it. He is more traditional, more conser-
> vative. But we have *always* argued and been at odds, so it wasn't the first time
> that I was doing something and believing in something that he was against. . . .
> When I went home for that first vacation, he just did not talk about it and neither
> did I. . . . He was against it when I told him that I was getting married. Once he

met Syd though, he couldn't help liking her. I think that he thinks of her like a daughter now. . . . They all love her.

On the other end of the spectrum, Kris's parents have disowned him since he came out as gay four years ago. Kris shared,

I was respectful of my parents' wishes for me the whole time that I was still at home, including when I was in college. I did not date men, and I occasionally went out on dates with girls to please them. But when I left home and had my own roof over my head, I thought that it was time to start living my life as my true self. That was when I met Sam. I was still in Atlanta, and he was in Massachusetts. After we had been dating for about six months, I found a job, a good job, near Sam's job, and we found an apartment together. That is when I came out to my parents. All hell broke loose. My mother started screaming that it was the work of Lucifer. My father told me to take my things and get out of the house. They started quoting the Bible that I was sinning. . . . I called the next day, and they told me that they wanted me to go to counseling so that I would stop being gay. I told my mother that it would not work, and she hung up on me. . . . Since then, I have tried to talk to them, but they say that I am a sinner. They still do not want to see me or to allow me to visit my brother and sister. I saw them before I moved, but they had to sneak to see me. We [he and his parents] will talk on the phone for a few minutes before the topic comes up, and then everything falls to pieces.

The most common reaction is for parents to be surprised by the news and to react somewhat negatively at first. With varying lengths of time though, most parents come to accept their child's disclosed sexual orientation. Mothers and fathers sometimes have different reactions, but it is more common for them to respond similarly. For example, Alan said that he and his wife, Helen, were at first inconsolable. He explained,

At first you feel like all of your hopes and dreams for your child have fallen by the wayside in one fell swoop. We wanted her to get married, have kids, buy a house . . . the whole nine yards. But when she told us that she was a lesbian, we thought that she would never have those things. We went into mourning. We were not mad at her, not angry at her. We were just upset that we were never going to be able to stop worrying about her, that she would never be [financially] independent of us. [Also an older parent, Alan assumed that only by marrying a man would his daughter be financially secure. He did not consider that both his daughter and his daughter's female partner might make an adequate income.] That is when we got involved with PFLAG [Parents and Friends of Lesbians and Gays], and it really helped. We met parents with the same concerns. Mostly though, we got mad at society for discriminating against gays and lesbians. So we got on the bandwagon and went to the [gay pride] parades and marches for marriage. We have become big advocates for gay rights. My daughter says now that we are more gay than they are. We still go to PFLAG, but now to help other parents. . . . It took us about six months to get used to the idea. Now we think of Karen like another daughter, and it is killing us that they are separated.

Alan said that despite Libby and Karen eventually being able to marry, he still feels distraught that Libby will never have the financial security that she would have with a husband. Likewise, he knows that Libby and Karen could adopt a child (or one of them be artificially inseminated) and that they could buy a house. Instead, they have chosen not to have a child and to live in an apartment, which he sees as less secure. This example suggests that a parent's concerns about a homosexual child are often a response to outdated assumptions; expectations of a nuclear family for that child inclusive of a mother, father, children, and home; and a belief that it is only this family formation that is "normal." This would suggest that parents may become ambivalent, having negative as well as positive emotions for their homosexual children, given earlier findings that ambivalence arises when children do not reach expected life markers.[11]

Mothers are more likely than fathers to be embarrassed that their child is homosexual or to be worried about what others will say. Sally said,

Once I got used to it myself, I thought, "Oh, God, how am I going to tell my mother?" She and my son have such a nice relationship, and I did not want to ruin it. . . . She was fine with it though. She just said, "Well, that is okay." And that was the last that she said of it. My own brother and sister were supportive of me, of us. We have all gotten used to it. . . . My husband . . . he was actually okay with it from the start, which surprised me.

Susan, the mother of Tyler, said,

I felt that it was my fault when he [Tyler] told me. I thought, "Now everyone is going to think that I am a bad mother." . . . I raised a gay son, so what does that make me? [I then asked how her husband reacted.] Jeff was okay with it. . . . He was always closer to our other son, who is more of a jock. Tyler was my son though. . . . I realized that I was the mother of a gay son, one of those women that I always felt sorry for.

Highly religious parents are also more likely to react negatively when their child discloses his or her sexual orientation. Samantha's parents, who are Anglican, and Nancy's mother, who is Catholic, initially had a very difficult time accepting their child's sexual orientation. Samantha's parents wanted her to see a priest and undergo therapy to "change back" to a heterosexual, a process that is discredited today. It took several months for each to begin talking to their child again and to become open to accepting their child's identity. Maria's parents, Hispanic and Catholic, and Kris's parents, Pentecostal, were still unwilling to talk to their children about their sexuality but instead quoted the Bible and told their children that they were sinning. They insisted that their children renounce their homosexuality and accept God "again" in their lives. Both children insisted they were still the children of God but could not reject who they were. Kris replied by also quoting passages from the Bible that he believed supported God and Jesus's acceptance of homosexuality. These conversations have not changed his parents' perspective though to date. Thus, both religion and ethnicity may influence a parent's reaction to the news that their child is gay.

Being in the military also affects how a parent responds, particularly to a son announcing that that he is gay. Connie said that her own husband has not been able to accept their son's homosexuality. She believes that it is because of the time that her husband spent in the army as a very young man when gay men were treated very badly and routinely harassed by their fellow soldiers. She said, "He just can't get past the idea that being gay is queer, a faggot. He won't say it, but he thinks that our son is a faggot." Connie's husband, Tony, has dealt with his son's news by ignoring it and putting it in the back of his mind. He treats Ben as he always has, but he has also told him to never bring one of his "friends" to their home. (This will be discussed in greater detail in chapter 3.)

The adult children said that they were most concerned that their parents would be disappointed in them when they came out. One daughter said, "I felt the same way that I did when I told my parents that I was dropping out of college. I just knew that they would be disappointed and that it would take them a while to get used to [it]. . . . I just really dreaded that look that was on their faces." Another son added, "Look, no one wants to have these intense conversations with your parents. You don't want to have to get into this sort of thing . . . have to talk things out. I just dreaded having to go through it more than anything. I wasn't all that worried about the outcome." A few, however, said that they had actually been afraid that their parents would disown them. These were most likely situations where the parents were deeply religious.

Some adult children never actually "came out of the closet" to their parents. Charlotte, for example, never told her parents that she was a lesbian. She shared,

I suppose that at some level my parents knew. My father worked with a woman
who lived with another woman, and I suppose he may have surmised that they
were a couple. . . . I announced that Natalia and I were buying a house together,
and later I announced that we were adopting. They just never asked, and I never
revealed anything. . . . Natalia's mother did ask me once though what my inten-
tions were towards her daughter. . . . I told [Natalia] that her mother wanted
to know the status of our relationship. She just said, "Mother, we are lovers."
Evelyn said, "I knew that. I don't know why you didn't just say so earlier."

BECOMING THE PARENT OF A GAY OR LESBIAN CHILD

The process of redefining what it means to be the parent of a gay or lesbian
child involves multiple steps, some of which may occur simultaneously and
some of which must occur sequentially. Parents may not even complete all of
the steps but instead get "stuck" in the process and never become comfortable
fully in their new role. Based on the experiences of the parents in this study,
redefining what it means to be the parent of a gay or lesbian child includes
the following steps:

1. Being open to your child's disclosure that he or she is gay
2. Realizing that you are not a "bad parent"
3. Digesting the information and literature on homosexuality
4. Changing your definition of what it means to be gay or lesbian (if previously inaccurate)
5. Rethinking who your child is
6. Fully integrating your child's spouse/partner into the family equally with
   your other children-in-law
7. Becoming an advocate for your child's rights

Step 1: Being Open to Your Child's
Disclosure that He or She Is Gay

Becoming the parent of a gay or lesbian child is a long-term process. It often
begins with the children declaring their sexual orientation, or "coming out,"
but may also originate when the parents begin to intuit that their child is
homosexual. Thus it usually starts when the child is a teenager or young adult
but may occur when they are middle aged. Very few parents actually reject
their child over the long term. These parents are never open to the possibility
of accepting their child's homosexuality. For that reason, the first stage in the
process involves being open to the child's disclosure that he or she is gay or

a lesbian. Samantha offers a good example of how this process may unfold. Consider her experience:

> I told my parents the first summer that I went home after meeting Shannon. I was really dreading it because my parents are very religious. I decided to tell them after dinner. . . . They were shocked. There were lots of tears. My mother just started crying. My father wanted me to see a priest. Then my mother started looking up on the Internet about something she had seen on TV about therapies that have been shown to transform people to hetero. . . . When we went to bed, everyone was still crying, but both of my parents were saying [they] still loved me, and it was okay. . . . *Then, in the morning*, they were rock solid that I was a sinner and that I absolutely had to go into counseling. Again with the priest . . . and they were adamant that it was all due to me studying abroad, that it would not have happened if I had not lived [elsewhere]. There was no crying, no acceptance. They did not want to talk about it anymore. . . . The rest of the visit was awful. It was just a few more days, but it seemed like eternity. I did not call them for several weeks. When finally I did, they still did not want to talk about it. I started to dread calling them . . . so I stopped. It was like that for about twelve weeks.

Samantha believes that it was about three months after her disclosure to her parents that she was homosexual that they began to open up to the possibility that she was a lesbian. She shared the following:

> My mom e-mailed me and told me that she and my dad were trying to accept it and that I needed to be patient. . . . We had a few e-mails back and forth. She explained that what I was doing was against their religion and that was hard for them to accept. Then she started saying that she still loved me and wanted what was best for me, even if they could not agree with it. . . . That was really the starting point for me, when I realized that they [were] opening up to accepting it.

Samantha began calling her parents again after several months of e-mail exchanges. Six months later, her parents traveled to Samantha and Shannon's house and stayed for a three-week visit. Samantha stated that the visit was sometimes stressful. She also said though that it was at this visit that her parents came to care for Shannon and to recognize Shannon and Samantha's genuine love for one another.

Step 2: Realizing that You Are Not a "Bad Parent"

Susan was concerned but open to her son's news when he announced he was gay during a summer visit from college. However, her second reaction to his

disclosure was to feel she had failed as a parent. Although she said she understood intellectually that it had nothing to do with the way she and her husband
had raised Tyler, she still "felt in her heart" that his "choice" to be gay was a
reflection of her. Susan said, "I just kept going over and over, what mistake
could I have made? Did I coddle him too much? Was his rejection of women
really a rejection of me? Why was one son gay and the other not? Hadn't I
treated them both the same?" What helped Susan to understand that she was
not responsible for her son being gay was the literature that he gave to her on
homosexuality. In particular, she learned that sexual orientation is not a choice
and not a rejection of her. Likewise, she started to attend PFLAG meetings and
found that there were other parents who were also struggling to accept their
children's sexuality. They were respectable men and women much like herself
and her husband. Susan said it was then that she began to realize that having
a gay or lesbian child could, and did, happen to anyone. And it was only then
that she began to "let herself off the hook" for her son's sexual orientation.

Step 3: Digesting the Information and Literature on Homosexuality

Adult children often give their parents pamphlets or books on homosexuality
to dispel any myths, including the myth that it is a choice. Parents begin to
process the information and literature only after they have opened themselves
up to the possibility of their child being gay or lesbian versus turning their
child away or refusing to accept it. Sometimes this happened in conjunction
with understanding that their child's sexual orientation was not their fault. In
other situations, it occurred afterward. Alan and Helen explained,

> It took a couple of months for it to sink in. . . . It is just a very slow process to
> digest it, to hear it. It is so foreign to what you have assumed for your child's
> whole life, even earlier. I started to think at that point, "Well, at least she isn't
> transsexual." I just thought about how things could be so much worse. Mostly
> though, I just had to sit with the information for a couple of months.

Lisa also added,

> You have to process it, what it means. It is like you go through a list. "Okay, he
> is gay. That means he is not going to have kids . . . that there is not going to be
> a pretty church wedding with your new daughter-in-law, and I [won't] have to
> help her pick out the dress." Then I started to think, "Okay, he is going to bring a
> young man home at some point, *his* young man. They might hold hands or kiss,
> and I will need to not react. It means that I am going to have to tell my parents."
> You just have to let it all sink in.

Step 4: Changing Your Definition of What It Means to Be Gay or Lesbian

It was at this point in the process, and sometimes in conjunction with the other steps, that parents began to learn more about the gay and lesbian community. Some met their child's partner or boyfriend/girlfriend for the first time. Parents whose children had previously introduced their boyfriend/girlfriend as "just a friend" realized that the new partners were no different from heterosexuals. Kim said that her mom was surprised to learn that her first girlfriend was not "butch" but was instead as feminine as her heterosexual friends. This was a relief for Kim's mother who did not want to have a masculine daughter-in-law. Likewise, Susan met Tyler's new boyfriend and liked him from the start. She said, "I was just so afraid that he was going to be like the stereotypical gay man. My stomach was doing somersaults for the whole week before we met him. But when I saw him in the restaurant, I just breathed a sigh of relief because he wasn't what I had feared."

Other parents explained that this was the point they started to tell their family members their son or daughter was gay or lesbian. Connie stated,

> I decided to tell my mother and father before they found out some other way. . . . Plus I just needed to tell someone else. My husband wasn't hearing any of it, and I needed someone to vent to. . . . I could tell from their expressions that they felt the way that I did (like they were devastated too), but they said that it was okay and they still loved him anyway. . . . The next time that we visited, they acted like everything was the same. Then I told my sisters, and they were like, "Oh, well, so-and-so's son is gay too, and really it is going to be fine." So the worst of my fears were over. . . . I told some of my closest girlfriends, and they didn't even blink. So, I figured, well, maybe it is okay . . . being gay.

Other parents said that they started to notice gay characters on television and that more and more public figures were announcing that they were gay. Another mother said, "I just realized that it was everywhere. I am not saying that I was happy about it, but I realized that it was okay." Alan said that after he started to do research, he became convinced his daughter would not get AIDS from her partner. Only then could he begin to see his daughter's lesbian identity in a positive light.

At this stage, parents begin to see homosexuality as within the boundaries of what is acceptable. They may not yet be able to challenge the assumptions that their child will be heterosexual, but they no longer see a gay or lesbian lifestyle as highly deviant or "wrong." At this point, parents are no longer alarmed by their child's sexual orientation.

28 Chapter 2

Step 5: Rethinking Who Your Child Is

Once parents begin to have a more positive definition of what it means to be gay or lesbian, they are able to view their child positively as well. Then parents begin to see their child in a new light. They start to reinterpret their son or daughter's history and to reimagine their future. Connie explained,

> A light bulb went off. I started to understand why he never went to dances, why he was so particular about the way that he looked, and why he seemed so different from his brother and father. . . . Then I started to think about what the future held for him. He's gay. He's not going to settle down with a pretty girl and have kids. . . . He told me that he was part of a large group of . . . others like him, never just one boyfriend. So I started to think that maybe he will just stay single. . . . Maybe he will just always be the single uncle in the family who whisks in at the holidays to be with everyone. . . . One of my uncles is like that, and he seems happy enough.

Alan added,

> Your dreams go up in smoke. Your little girl is never going to have the life that you wanted for her. But I started to think about what her life will be like, and what that will mean for my life and Sally's [life]. . . . We can still have grandkids and bounce them on our knee. They just may not look like us. We can still go to her house for Christmas dinner. A lot of that isn't going to change. I worry though that her future won't be financially secure, that I will still have to be responsible for her financially. I will have to retire later than I want to, which is a problem because I'm tired.

As parents began to redefine the events of their child's life and to reimagine their future, they also began to develop a new definition of who their child was. Sally said, "I see Kyle differently now. I am not saying that I look down on him or think negatively about him. But I realize that he is not the boy that I had made up in my mind. . . . He is a grown man who is going to have to face a lot of challenges in life, and I have to accept who he is and be there for him, help him to face them." Likewise, Sharon explained, "I had to accept that my daughter is never going to be the girly girl that I always wanted. That it is more than the fact that she doesn't like to wear dresses. She is the man in that family, the assertive one. And I need to accept that."

Thus, many parents developed a new image of their child in their mind as they processed becoming the parent of that child. They also stated they had to remind themselves that their child was, in other ways, still the same person they had always loved. Lisa shared,

I accepted what my son was doing and who he was. Yes, I saw him somewhat differently than I had. But I also realized that he was still the same old Connor. I could still see that sweet, sensitive little boy who came home with scrapes and scratches because the other boys had pushed him and made fun of him. He was *always* going to need me to be in his corner because that was who he was and who he would always be.

Connie said, "It was a relief that first month after he came out to still be able to joke about things. He was still the same kid. He was still my boy even though he was gay."

Step 6: Fully Integrating Your Child's Partner/Spouse into the Family

Adult children want their families to include their spouses and to treat them similarly to the other children-in-law in the family. Parents are more likely to do this once they have redefined what it means to be gay or lesbian and have begun to see homosexuality as within the boundaries of what is expected in our society. It requires though that the parent accept the child as being gay or lesbian and not deny his or her sexual orientation. This is usually the greatest barrier to a parent including their new same-sex son-in-law or daughter-in-law in the family.

Barb's mother has never accepted her spouse, Marie, into the family. Before they married, Barb took Marie to meet her parents for the weekend. Barb said that both her mother and her father ignored Marie for the entire weekend. Although they have been together as a couple for thirteen years and have been married for ten years, Barb's mother Renee sends holiday cards and gifts solely to her daughter. Nor does Renee ask about Marie or their two children (both of whom were carried by Marie) when Barb calls her. Renee tells her friends that Barb has "adopted" two children, a term that Barb finds insulting. Renee does not send the children birthday gifts or otherwise acknowledge them. As a result of her wife and children not being included in the family, Barb calls her mother every four months and visits her only every seven years.

Parents who had accepted their children's sexuality were usually willing to treat their spouses similar to the other children-in-law. Typically, they related to the spouses based on their gender: lesbian spouses were treated like daughters-in-law, and gay spouses were treated like sons-in-law. Charlotte though said that her in-laws, especially her father-in-law, treated her like a son-in-law. That is, they treated their daughter's wife like a man. Charlotte said,

Natalia's sister-in-law and Natalia would usually help their mother in the kitchen around mealtime, but her father would always invite me out to barbeque. . . . He would also share with me their financial situation and ask my advice, . . . and he would complain about my mother-in-law to me. . . . It was the typical way that he treated other men, but he did not privy Natalia or her sister-in-law. I never quite knew how to respond.

This suggests that parents may be eager to include their child's spouse in the family but still be unclear about the role that the person will have or the myriad ramifications of having a child in a same-sex marriage.

Step 7: Becoming an Advocate for Your Child's Rights

Many parents eventually become advocates for gay and lesbian rights. Alan and Helen were highly involved in the GLBT community and had once led the local PFLAG association. They marched in gay pride parades and picketed the state house for the passage of same-sex marriage. Nancy's mother, Arlene, was also a parent-turned-advocate. Arlene first refused to talk to Nancy when she announced her commitment to Sue. According to Nancy though, her mother is now one of the most vocal promoters of GLBT rights. She said, "My mother will say to me, 'Guess what so-and-so said [referring to something about homosexuality]?' Then she'll say, 'But I told him that was ignorant. I told him he was being an ass. Can you imagine being so Neanderthal?'"

Not all parents become advocates for gay and lesbian rights. Some get stuck in the phase of redefining what it means to be gay or lesbian. Usually these parents are still concerned about what others will think if they have a homosexual child because they continue to see homosexuality as highly deviant. Many of these parents have not heard positive societal reactions or have limited exposure to gay and lesbian individuals. These parents are referred to as "stuck in the family closet."

CHANGING FAMILY SYSTEMS

Adult children disclosing their homosexuality to the family affects not only their individual relationships with others but the entire family system as well.[12] In some families, "sides" develop between those who accept the child's sexuality and those who do not. Kris, for example, said that his brothers and sisters were very angry at their parents for rejecting him.

Likewise, his parents were upset with their other children for being in contact with Kris. Kris's brother told him that they argue with their parents whenever his name comes up. Likewise, Shay said that her father and biological siblings support her lesbianism, but her stepsiblings do not. As a result, her brother and sister have less to do with their stepsiblings than in the past. Parents also become estranged from their own brothers and sisters or other extended family members who are not accepting of their children. The extent to which they remove themselves from their family members' lives depends on how open the person is in his or her disapproval. For example, Nancy's uncle is a priest. When Nancy announced her relationship with another woman in her annual Christmas letter, her uncle told her mother, Arlene, that he did not approve but that he would say no more to Nancy. Although Nancy is somewhat uncomfortable around her uncle, it has not affected her mother's relationship with her brother. However, Arlene told Nancy that her aunt had said some "horrific" things in an e-mail after Nancy came out and that she and her sister were no longer in touch because of that.

Friction between parents can intensify when they disagree on how to react to their child's news. Connie said that she and Tony were already having marital difficulties when their son Ben came out. Connie was supportive of Ben, but she felt that Tony was not. Connie said that things between them grew much worse when Tony told his son that his boyfriends were not welcome in their home. Connie said, "I just couldn't see saying that to him. It wasn't right. This is his home. It was just another example of my husband being inflexible. . . . It ended up being the straw that broke the camel's back. We just continued to argue about it. . . . We separated about six months later." In contrast, Barb tries to talk to her husband about accepting their son, but it has not resulted in any real conflict between them. Barb said that she and her husband do not argue about the matter, but neither will her husband change his mind on the subject.

Having a family member come out of the closet results in further diversification in the family. It encourages other family members to feel comfortable to explore new avenues. Ben said that his cousin came out of the closet shortly after he did. He said, "I think that she would have had to come out anyway, but this made it easier. I kind of paved the way. I think that no one looked at her the same way that they [look at] me because I came out first. . . . I think that they might have expected it about her, but they did not expect it about me." In other families, siblings began dating—and some eventually married—people of other races. Susan said, "We joke that I opened the door for my sister to marry a black man. If my parents were accepting of me marrying

a woman, then surely they would not mind her marrying a black man. . . .
Sure enough, it did not have near the impact that it would have had before I
got married."

In sum, most adult children reveal their sexual orientation to their parents
in a process referred to as "coming out." Parents are surprised and concerned
about the difficulties that their children will have to overcome. Many believe
that their dreams for their child are shattered in that moment, dreams of what
they consider to be a normal life. Adult children worry that their parents will
be disappointed in them as a result. A minority of parents rejects their child
at that point, although most come to accept their child's sexual orientation.
The process of redefining themselves as the parent of a gay child is a lengthy
process that includes learning what it means to be gay or lesbian and rethinking who your child is. It involves redefining your child's past and reimaging
his or her future as well. For many, the entire family system changes as a
result of this pivotal event. The next chapter will focus on the quality of the
relationship between parents and their gay or lesbian child. It will give parents some idea of the kind of relationship they may have with their child, what
determines the differences, and the vast array of experiences.

Chapter 3

Relationships between Parents and Their Gay or Lesbian Children

The purpose of this chapter is to provide parents with a primer on the type and quality of relationships that parents typically have with their gay or lesbian children. Relationships between parents and their married adult children run the gamut from "tight knit" (characterized by high affection, opportunities to see one another, and an exchange of resources) to "detached" (ones that offer little affection, opportunity to see one another, or exchange of resources).[1] Most parent-and-child bonds are generally positive and reflect a high level of unanimity on multiple dimensions.[2] This does not preclude relationships from experiencing conflict and ambivalence as well though.

There are significant differences in intergenerational ties based on gender. Unlike sons, daughters are more likely to have the aforementioned "tight-knit" relationships as well as "obligatory" relationships with their parents, which are characterized by low levels of affection but high levels of opportunity to see one another and exchange resources. This suggests that daughters remain close to their parents, even when they have little affection for them.[3] They, along with their husbands, are also more likely to exchange resources with her parents than with his parents.[4] Overall, there is greater contact with the wife's side of the family than the husband's side of the family.

There is some evidence for the popular adage, "A son is a son till he takes him a wife, a daughter is a daughter all of her life." That is, daughters tend to remain close to their parents following marriage while sons are somewhat more detached from their parents.[5] However, the differences are not as large as one might expect. It may be that daughters continue to remain close to their parents following marriage because of strong normative expectations to do so. In addition, there is a great deal of overlap between their roles as daughter

33

and wife/mother, such as facilitating the relationship between grandparent and grandchild. Sons, however, are not expected to remain close to parents. Many sons feel obligated to focus more on the provider role and their careers following marriage, although they still remain somewhat close to parents. Unlike their wives, there is not as great an overlap between their roles of son and husband/father. Wives are also more likely to be the ones who set the couple's social calendar and tend to draw their husbands more into their own families, while husbands do neither. Thus, the effect of marriage on parent–adult child relationships is gendered: sons step back from their families of origin following marriage while daughters do not. However, the effect is not as strong as we assume.

Some parents though do feel that they lose their sons following marriage. This is more likely when parents do not get along well with their daughters-in-law. Mothers feel as though they are on the outside (of their son's life) looking into it. These sons might occasionally visit their parents without their wives; others might visit with their wives but do so even more rarely. Usually these couples try to maintain cordial relationships with the husband's parents, but there is always an undercurrent of tension and sometimes outright hostility. Sons say that there have been times in their marriages when they felt as though they had to choose between their parents and their spouses because of the estranged relationships, but all prioritized their marriages. In these instances, relationships with the husband's parents tend to wax and wane over time.[6]

These earlier studies were conducted on the general population or focused exclusively on heterosexual couples. It is important to investigate the quality of intergenerational relationships for children in same-sex relationships as well though, particularly as more and more young men and women disclose their homosexual identity. Parent–adult child relationships are an important source of psychological well-being for both generations and may impact marriage, general health, and parental caregiving in later life.[7] There may be need for support and interventions for these families. For this reason, this next section focuses on the quality of parent–adult child relationships for gay and lesbian adult children.

There are a number of reasons the quality of parent–adult children relationships will differ when children are gay or lesbian. The fact that homosexuality is still relatively "new" to a family when they find out and not accepted by everyone will likely result in ambivalence (the existence of both positive and negative emotions) among parents. Parents may be embarrassed by their child's sexual orientation or disappointed that their children are not following the dream that they had set for them. These children's earliest expression of their sexual orientation or difficult discussions when they came out of the closet may continue to affect the relationship. Children's affection for parents may also be diminished as a result of the parents' embarrassment. Of all family relationships, parents and children are most likely to love one another unconditionally though. For all of these reasons, it is expected that parent–adult child relationships will be highly complicated when children are gay or lesbian.

THE QUALITY OF PARENT–ADULT CHILD RELATIONSHIPS

Similar to studies in the general population, the majority of parents and homosexual adult children describe their relationship with one another very positively. More often than not, both parents and adult children hesitated in their descriptions or offered some disclaimer that the relationship could be even stronger still if there had not been some conflict surrounding the adult child's sexuality. They were not as enthusiastic or overwhelmingly positive as the mothers of heterosexual children or the heterosexual children themselves in their corresponding descriptions. For example, Samantha explained,

> Yes, my parents and I are very close again. I call every week. They always ask about Aimee. . . . They e-mail both of us. My sister Skypes us both now. They have come a long way. . . . Still though, it is not the way that it *was* [prior to her coming out]. I can't forget what happened, the things they said. . . . Plus, sometimes they just say the most ridiculous things. Like, last week I told my dad that I was going on vacation. He said, "Aimee too?" He would not have asked my sister if my brother-in-law was going with her on vacation. . . . It makes me think that they have not really accepted that we are married, like other people.

In contrast, heterosexual children are much less likely to qualify their relationships with parents because they are not affected by such conflict. Marie, who is heterosexual, for example, shared the following about her relationship with her parents:

> My dad is deceased now, but I have always been very close to both parents. I see my mom usually every other day, sometimes every day. She lives the next street over. I pick her up when I go shopping. She will stop by with produce that she gets at the farm stand. We have her over on Sundays, or she goes with us and the kids for the day. . . . My husband is closer to my family than his own. He just got a promotion, and we had his party at my parents' house [versus his parents' house, which is also in the area]. We are just a close family. . . . I can talk to my

mom about anything. . . . We have similar personalities and usually see things the same way. . . . My kids go over there on their bikes anytime.

Likewise, another heterosexual daughter said, "My mom and I are extremely close. We talk on the phone usually every day. . . . We talk mostly about the kids, about work. She knows what is going on in our family at all times. If I need help with the kids, she will be over on the dime. . . . We take her with us on vacations and on family outings. . . . I know that she always has my back and would do anything for my kids."

The very best of the relationships between parents and heterosexual children are much less likely to be qualified in comparison to the very best of the relationships between parents and homosexual children. Only a minority of homosexual children describes their relationships with parents without some proviso. Emily was one of those daughters. She summarized her relationship with her mother as such: "It is wonderful. My mother is the sweetest, kindest person that I can imagine. She is tolerant and accepting, thoughtful and kind. . . . She is very family oriented and loves our children. I feel very close to her, although not in the sense of best friends. . . . I would do anything for her. . . . I always felt very loved." Emily, however, has never discussed or disclosed her sexual orientation with either of her parents, which may have accounted for the lack of negative repercussions. More typical were comments such as Kim's: "My relationship with my mother is fine. She loved, loved, loved my first girlfriend, but I can tell that she is not as happy with my wife, who is more masculine. It doesn't affect my relationship with my mother too much . . . except that there are things that I would not share with her, and I don't spend a lot of time with both Pam and my mother." And then there's Ed's example:

> I am very close to my family. We go there about once a month, for the weekend, but only because of my schedule. It used to be every other weekend. We hang out and do things together, go out to dinner together. My relationship with my dad used to be strained though . . . it is much less so now though. I just thought he loved my brother more because he is more into sports and stuff. . . . I still feel it a little bit—now and then.

As this example suggests, homosexual children were more likely to stipulate qualifications even in the best of relationships.[8] Thus, bonds between heterosexual children and parents were usually a step above those of gay and lesbian children and their parents.

Parents remain somewhat uncomfortable with their child's sexuality even in good relationships. For example, Connie said, "Yes, my son and I are very close. I went to their wedding . . . saw the house [that] they bought. My son comes to visit. . . . You know, you love your children no matter what. . . . I am closer to my daughter though. There isn't anything standing between us—no elephant in the room."

Sometimes parents come to accept their children's homosexuality and their partner only after they are married. One daughter explained,

> Our marriage made a big difference for my mother. . . . Marriage is important to her. I think that she realized that my marriage is not that different from her marriage . . . or my sister's marriage. The fact that it is legal, binding. . . . Plus, she saw that all of these other people [meaning the wedding guests] were supportive, even my grandmother. She saw how supportive [Jane's] family was, and I think that she felt a little guilty [that she had not been supportive before]. We had a commitment ceremony well before that, but it did not make a difference for her. . . . It just wasn't as meaningful to her.

Another mother said, "I was just so relieved that he found someone . . . someone who is strong and who clearly loves him. When he first came out, I did not think that he would ever have that. . . . When they said their "'I dos,' it was like a flood of relief just washed over me. I was so grateful—to my son-in-law for that."

More of the homosexual married children had alienated or displaced relationships with their parents than was true of the heterosexual children and their parents. This included gay and lesbian adults who had only very infrequent phone conversations with their parents because their parents would not accept their sexuality. These parents did not come to their children's weddings and had not met their spouses. Conversations would turn into arguments over the phone if the child tried to discuss the topic. Several of the parents were highly religious, and they would quote Bible phrases that undermined homosexuality whenever their child brought up the topic. Kris, for example, said,

> It has been about four years now since I told them about Sam. I still can't even bring up the topic without it turning into a huge fight. . . . I sent them a wedding invitation, but they never even said anything about it. I know that my brother and sister would have come if they could have. . . . They told me to stay away until I bring God back into my life, which to them means that I renounce being gay, like I could even do that. . . . I've studied the Bible too. I can quote passages where it is clear that Jesus does accept homosexuals, but they say I am being blasphemous. They want me to divorce Sam and move back [home] and just forget everything that I have built, but I cannot go back to that life . . . where I pretended to be something I wasn't.

Likewise, Maria talked to her parents on the telephone infrequently. They told her that she was welcome to visit but that she could not bring her wife with her. Maria told them that she would not visit without her spouse. Parents continue to have contact with their children because of the unconditional love between them though. Still, they are not able to accept their child's homosexuality or spouse.

Fewer of the heterosexual children were estranged from their parents. Estrangement occurred most often when there was conflict between one's parents and spouse. One child had limited contact with his father due to his father's history of alcoholism. In all of these cases though, the children still occasionally visited their parents and talked to them on the phone. They might not have visited as often as they would have otherwise, but the conflict was much more contained than it was between homosexual children and the parents who did not accept them. For example, one of the heterosexual sons said,

> I don't see my parents regularly because my wife doesn't want to see them. She is convinced that they do not like her. . . . I don't know if they do or don't anymore. . . . So we don't see them on holidays even though we live in the same state. . . . I go over to see them sometimes after work. It is awkward. I know that they want me to stick up for them, and they are mad that I don't. It is just not a good situation.

Likewise, Bruce occasionally saw his alcoholic father despite his anger toward him. In contrast though, several of the homosexual children have not seen their parents in years because of the conflict surrounding their homosexuality.

Some of the lesbian and gay children occasionally see their parents, but their marriages are a source of great contention. Barb visits her mother who lives several states away every seven years, but no more often, because her mother does not ask about her wife or their children. In some instances, it is only one of the parents who does not accept the marriage, but the child ends up spending less time with both parents as a result. Ben said, "I don't go and visit because my father does not want me to bring Casey. Sometimes I go by myself [to visit], but not very often . . . because of that." As a result, Ben does not see his mother very often either. Steve said that his mother would probably be more accepting of his husband and sexual orientation if it were not for his highly homophobic stepfather. Likewise, Steve feels that his stepfather belittles him because of his sexuality, so he visits his mother only once a year. He calls his mother only occasionally because he resents the fact that his mother never stood up for him when his stepfather bullied him as a child. Steve said, "My [step]father used to take me to the ball field . . . to butch me up . . . it was almost abusive. . . . My mother never stepped in, but I think that she should have."

The fact that one set of the couple's parents are often much more accepting than the other set of parents means that homosexual couples spend a disproportionately greater amount of time with one set of parents than the other, relative to heterosexual couples. For example, Ed said, "I came out when I was twenty-two, over twenty years ago. My parents have had a long time to get used to it . . . and they did. They have met all of my boyfriends. Phil's parents have met only me. . . . It is a lot more comfortable with my parents, so we go there a lot more than we would otherwise." In contrast, heterosexual children are much more likely to at least try to balance the time that they spend with each set of parents, unless there is significant conflict. One of the heterosexual daughters said, "We spend more time with my parents, yes. We live far away and I miss my family very much. So we spend more of our vacation time with them. But . . . we go see my in-laws too, and they are always welcome to come here, which they do. I make sure that they know their grandchildren and get to see us every summer and Christmas."

Interestingly, those adult children who never come out of the closet to their parents usually have very good relationships with them. Charlotte commented,

> I would say that I had a wonderful relationship with my parents. They adored our children. . . . I was fortunate that they expected us [meaning she and her sister] to have careers . . . and therefore needed good educations and intellectual stimulation . . . at a time when that was not very popular for girls. They were always supportive of anything that I wanted. They gave us money to adopt our children and helped us to buy this house. . . . I think that they knew that Natalia and I were a couple . . . how could they not? It just wasn't something that I thought they would want to have spoken about. . . . I did not want to bludgeon them with it.

Thus, Charlotte was accepting of the fact that she could not announce her marriage to her parents, as long as they embraced the unspoken reality.

Some of the adult children moved far from their parents because of their sexuality. Ben said, "My father was so against it. I felt like I couldn't be myself if I lived anywhere near him. So I moved as far away as possible. I don't see as much of my parents now, but at least I don't have to be looking over my shoulder all the time." Kris and Bob live far from Kris's home state because of his parents' disapproval of their lifestyle. One of the older men said that he would never live in the same community as his own adult children because they are not aware of his marriage and will not find out as long as they live far away. Others did not move far away, but they were grateful that they lived in another geographic area so that they did not have to be as self-conscious when out in public with their partner.

SONS VERSUS DAUGHTERS

Fathers have greater difficulty accepting a son's sexual orientation than a daughter's. The definition of masculinity in our society is based on the heterosexual model. That is, masculine men have women by their side, not men. The cultural ideal is one of hypermasculinity. Real men are not only strong but very strong, and effeminate men are highly criticized. However, the stereotype of the gay man is that he is somewhat feminine, making it very difficult for fathers to accept their sons' homosexuality. It is the father's responsibility to impart masculinity, and fathers may feel they have let their sons down or that their gay sons have let themselves down. One of the mothers said, "My son is not only gay, but he is a drag queen as well. My ex-husband won't have anything to do with him because of it. He says that he has disowned him. . . . I think that he is just really embarrassed by the way that Michael dresses . . . and the fact that he goes out in public like that."

While most gay men do not fit an effeminate stereotype, the strength of the association continues to plague father-and-son relationships. Gay relationships and the act of anal intercourse are less accepted in society overall, making it harder for sons to come out of the closet. One of the fathers of a lesbian daughter said, "I just keep telling myself that at least she isn't trans[sexual]." Then later he added, "I suppose that I should be happy too that at least I'm dealing with a gay [lesbian] situation [versus her being transsexual]." Likewise, Lisa pointed out that it had been extremely difficult for Connor while he was growing up because he was a dancer and was not excessively masculine. She said that even today, he gets looks of disapproval while on the subway. Lisa commented, "To whatever extent he looks gay, people harshly disapprove."

Lesbian women though are not as harshly judged. Homosexuality has traditionally been associated with sodomy, perhaps from the framing of laws and biblical scripture. In contrast, strong women are more accepted and regarded within a range of acceptable behavior. The stereotype of the "butch" lesbian is not as loathsome in our society as the effeminate gay man. While homophobia may prevent someone from embracing lesbianism, that person is still less likely to shun lesbianism than being gay.

Sons were more likely to have estranged relationships with their parents than daughters. While they wished that they were still in contact with their parents and hoped that their parents would eventually come to accept their homosexuality and their marriage, they were not willing to overlook their parents' homophobia. Bradley said, "I'm not going to bring [my husband] to my mother's place if he is not welcome, so I don't go either. She would be polite, but *I* would *know* that he wasn't welcome, so I don't go." Perhaps because sons feel less obligated to be in contact with parents than daughters, they are more likely to allow the estrangement to remain when there is conflict.[9]

Some of the men though did have good relationships with both of their parents. One of these sons, Ed, tried to live a heterosexual life when he was much younger. His parents were disappointed when he divorced his wife because he was gay, but they came to accept his sexuality. Men were more likely than women to attempt to suppress their homosexuality by first marrying someone of the opposite sex. The men said that they tried to "pass" as heterosexual, and thus were aware of their homosexuality. In contrast, the women who first lived as heterosexual said they did not realize they were lesbians until they were older. The shortest marriage lasted only a few years while one man managed to be married to his wife through most of his adult life. He did, however, have male lovers on and off throughout this period. Today, his adult children do not realize that he is gay or married to a man.

Women, however, were more sensitive to their parents' perspective on their marriages were than men. Sons were satisfied and accepted the situation as long as their parents did not outright reject them or their spouses. Daughters, though, were more concerned if their parents did not treat them similarly to their heterosexual siblings or offer complete acceptance. They were also more likely to hold back in their affection for their parents due to earlier expressions of disapproval. For example, Samantha said that although her parents have come a long way in accepting her and Aimee, the earlier statements that they made about the sinful nature of homosexuality still linger in her mind. Thus, although the relationship is better than it was, it will never be the same as it was originally. This gender difference reinforces earlier studies on the relative importance of relationships in general and family relationships in particular for women.[10]

Women tried to work with their parents more than sons did to gain their full acceptance. Those women whose parents were initially negative when they came out of the closet, or when they announced their intention to marry, exchanged countless e-mails, phone calls, or both with parents. They cried when their parents were not accepting and tried to reason with them to the best of their ability. If one parent was more accepting than the other, a daughter might seek that parent's assistance in soliciting the other parent's compliance. Rarely though did they ask their siblings or extended family to intervene. Daughters tried to point out that they could not change who they were even if they wanted to and expressed how much they wanted their parents to accept their circumstances. Daughters asked their parents just to meet their partner before making a decision or to read about homosexuality before denouncing it. Several of the daughters, but none of the sons, also sought the support of a therapist for themselves before coming out to their parents.

According to the literature, gay men do not necessarily become monogamous after they marry. This was investigated due to prior findings that unmarried gay men are less likely to be monogamous than unmarried lesbians.[11] It should be pointed out that straight married men, another reasonable comparison group, are not necessarily monogamous either. However, all of the married men in this study stated that they were monogamous even though they had not been monogamous in relationships previously. Married lesbians were also generally monogamous, but they had usually been in serial monogamous relationships prior to getting married. To this extent, marriage changes gay men's lives and relationships and is a transformative experience, as much and perhaps more so than is true for others. This will be discussed in greater detail in the following chapters.

MOTHERS VERSUS FATHERS

Fathers were more uncomfortable when their son was homosexual than when their daughter was homosexual. Mothers, however, were more fearful of their children's futures as a result of being homosexual. They worried that their sons or daughters would be discriminated against in the workplace and in society in general, that their sons would be assaulted, and that they would not be able to have children or be welcomed by some neighbors. Mothers said that they were concerned more about their homosexual children than their heterosexual children. Helen commented,

> I know that Libby and Karen can adopt a child, or have artificial insemination, but those things are expensive. Plus, what if she adopts a child with a learning disability or a medical problem? It would just be easier if she were in a

[heterosexual] marriage. . . . I think that the two of them in general are just less likely to settle down because they are lesbians. They are trying not to do traditional things, but those things also mean stability . . . like buying a house or living in the suburbs versus the big city. . . . Plus, I love Karen dearly, but she does not make as much money as a man would, and I worry about their finances. We have not retired yet because I worry that they may need our help.

Mothers were also more concerned about what others would think about their child's homosexuality. They were particularly concerned about what their own parents might think and how this would affect their parents' relationships with their children. This may have to do with mothers feeling greater responsibility for how their children turn out than do fathers. Especially for this generation of parents, parenting was primarily the mother's responsibility. Mothers were no more or less likely to accept their children's sexuality than were fathers when the child first came out of the closet.

Several of the daughters with elderly mothers were providing care for their moms at the time of the study. Despite any past or current tension, daughters volunteered to help a parent when needed. Two of the daughters went to their mother's home on a daily basis to provide personal care. Two other daughters monitored their mother's conditions daily by phone and flew out to help their parent whenever it was needed (as their employment allowed). One of these women said, "There is nothing that I would not do for her . . . despite any problems that we have had in our relationship in the past. I am totally devoted to her and will continue to do [i.e., be] so." Thus, filial obligation and the exchange that characterizes intergenerational relationships are so strong as to overcome all other differences when necessary; for these are the ties that bind.

WHAT MAKES A DIFFERENCE FOR THE QUALITY OF THE RELATIONSHIP?

Parents and adult children were more likely to enjoy positive close bonds if they also had good relationships prior to their child coming out of the closet. That is, parents and children were able to sustain their love and overcome any conflict when positive patterns of working out problems were established early on and when there was a prior high degree of affection for one another. One mother said, "I had to remind myself that he was still the same person that I had always loved. That did not change." Another mother said, "Our family always talks out its problems. We don't go to bed angry with one another. . . . Well, this was a more serious issue, but the principle is the same."

Highly educated and liberal parents were also more likely to accept their child's sexual orientation, which resulted in better relationships. Jackie's parents were highly progressive liberals who knew other gay and lesbian couples among their friends. It was therefore easier for them to accept Jackie's lesbian status. Betsy's father was not liberal, but he was highly educated. He understood that Betsy did not choose to be homosexual and was therefore not "responsible" for being a lesbian.

The very youngest of the adult children were more likely to describe very positive relationships with their parents. For example, one young son said, "My parents . . . they have been awesome about this. I could tell that I blew them over when I told them. They didn't lose it though. It was more like deer in the headlights. . . . My mom had a harder time understanding, accepting it. So I got some literature. A friend of ours told us about PFLAG meetings, and they were willing to go to those, which helped a lot." This suggests that there may be some generational difference in how parents respond. These parents were considerably younger than the oldest parents, who did not speak about their child's sexuality.

The inability of some parents to accept their child's sexuality may, in fact, be part of a generational gap between the parents and children. Many of the older parents were raised at a time in which interracial marriages were not allowed, and homosexuality was not even discussed. Divorce was stigmatized, and couples married if a woman was pregnant. For these parents, the heterosexual nuclear family was the only family formation that was acceptable. Such parents and adult children had a significant chasm to overcome in accepting one another's views. Several of these children though said that their parents had indeed come a long way in accepting their homosexuality. This is most likely due to the unconditional love that characterizes parent-and-child relationships. Parents, especially, will go to great lengths to maintain their relationships with their adult children.

In sum, the relationships between parents and their married lesbian and gay children run the gamut from being "tight knit" to "detached" or "estranged." Many of the tight-knit relationships though include caveats on the part of both parents and children as they recollect conflict regarding the child's sexuality from the past. Children often recalled prior hurt when their parents were not fully supportive. Parents continued to be disappointed that their children were not living the life that they had hoped for them. *Heterosexual* children though were more likely to be unequivocal in describing their closeness to their parents. Their lives were also more likely to be similar to their parents' lives than gay/lesbian children and their parents. Although many parents may come to accept their child's homosexuality over time, there is often some underlying tension from the earlier conflict. Relationships that were unaffected by the child's homosexuality were rare and usually occurred with highly liberal, well-educated parents.

Estranged relationships with parents are more common among the homosexual children than the heterosexual children. Estrangement for homosexual children was most often due to their parents' unwillingness to accept their sexual orientation, while estrangement for heterosexual children was more often the choice of the child and his or her spouse. Children whose parents did not accept their homosexuality had not seen their parents for several years, and conversations ended up in arguments over the phone. Heterosexual children who were estranged from their parents still saw them, and conflict was much more contained during conversations.

Even when children were ambivalent about their parents, they still provided care for them when necessary. Such is the strength of an adult child's obligation in our society. In addition, parents who were adamantly against their child's homosexuality to begin with often made great strides in coming to accept them due to the unconditional love that characterizes the relationship.

The fact that homosexuality is so hard for many parents to accept suggests how prevalent our expectations of heterosexuality are in our society. Parents who said that they were disappointed in their children grieved the loss of the dreams that they had for their kids, dreams that included a nuclear family with a husband and wife. Although their adult children could marry and adopt children, parents still saw such families as less desirable than a heterosexual family. However, younger parents were more likely to acquiesce than older parents, suggesting there may be a generational shift to greater acceptance of family alternatives. This is not surprising given the prevalence of other family structures in today's society to which younger generations of parents are accustomed, including single-parent families where the parent is either divorced or never married as well as an increase in adults living alone.

The next chapter looks at the effect of marriage on the relationship between parents and adult children so that parents may better understand how their relationships with children may or may not change after marriage. In particular, it will examine whether and how same-sex marriage improves or worsens relationships with one's parents and how that differs for sons versus daughters. The nature of the relationship between parents and children-in-law in same-sex marriages will also be investigated. The chapter will include a discussion of how same-sex marriage may be changing marriage in America and what that tells us about the social institution of marriage in the twenty-first century.

Chapter 4

The Effect of Same-Sex Marriage on Parent–Adult Child Relationships

The significant events or markers in one's life, such as starting college, marriage and divorce, having children, retirement, and so forth, all have an important impact on well-being and the remaining trajectory of life, including impacting relationships with other people. For example, the effects of divorce, either the parents' divorce or an adult child's divorce, on the parent and adult child's relationship have been well documented.[1] Interestingly, the absence of achieving life-course events also impacts intergenerational relationships. For example, the inability of adult children to reach important lifetime events, such as being employed or marrying, increases the likelihood of parents feeling ambivalent toward their children, or having both negative as well as positive regard for them.[2]

Marriage affects parent–adult child relationships in other ways as well because it is such a powerful institution and has such an all-encompassing effect on each spouse's life. In fact, it has been argued that because it is so all encompassing, marriage is actually a "greedy" institution that prevents spouses from maintaining other social ties and connections to the community.[3] The effect of marriage, however, differs for men versus women because marital roles differ so much for each and because the expectations of relationships with adult sons versus daughters are so different. In fact, the assumption of different relationships with married sons versus daughters is so prevalent in our society that we have the adage "A daughter is a daughter all of her life, but a son is a son 'til he takes him a wife."

In an earlier book, I questioned whether or not this saying is in fact an accurate portrayal of contemporary gender disparities by examining differences in married men versus married women's descriptions of their relationships with their parents as well as examining mothers' comparisons of their relationships with their married sons versus their married daughters.[4] This was the first analysis of the effects of marriage that took into account both children's and mothers' perspectives, thus providing a more comprehensive view. However, it looked exclusively at heterosexual marriage. This chapter examines whether or not the same holds true in same-sex marriage and whether and why there are any differences. As such, this chapter serves as a primer for parents on how their lesbian or gay child's marriage will impact their relationship with her or him.

This earlier book on heterosexual children finds that in fact there are some gender differences, but they are not as extensive as the above adage suggests.[5] Married heterosexual sons are a little more likely to step back from their relationships with parents following marriage than are married heterosexual daughters, according to both mothers and the sons. Mothers said that they had "lost" their sons to a greater degree than daughters because their attention was focused elsewhere after marriage. Sons were more likely to concentrate on their own families and careers following marriage and to be pulled into their spouse's family relative to daughters. In contrast, married daughters stayed close to their parents following marriage despite having careers as well.

The reasons for these gender differences are myriad. Heterosexual sons stated that they pulled back from their families of origin following marriage because they needed to focus on their careers and providing for their own families. They said that they still felt a part of their family of origin but that their own families now had to take priority. Heterosexual daughters, however, did not believe that they needed to focus any more or less on their careers following marriage, but they did feel an obligation to stay close to their parents. They believed that this expectation is common throughout society and not specific to their families. Their roles as wife and mother also overlapped with their responsibilities as daughter to a greater extent than men's roles as husband and father overlapped with their role as son. One of women's main obligations in the family is to be a conduit for their spouses' and children's relationships with other family members. Thus women can fulfill their role as mother while also spending time with their parents and bringing the two together. While sons sometimes brought their children to see their parents, it was not their central role as a father. Heterosexual men were more likely to expect their wives to facilitate that connection, even in the twenty-first century.

Sons also sometimes spent less time with their parents when their wives did not get along with their parents. Mothers were most likely to feel they had significantly "lost" their sons in these situations. In contrast, daughters continued to stay close to their parents even when their husbands did not get along well with their parents.

Daughters are also more likely to stay close to parents following marriage than sons because they are the ones who set the couple's social calendar. Even those women who tried to make things relatively equal with each set of parents said that they had a tendency to schedule more family time with their own parents than their husband's parents. Several of these women said that they just felt more comfortable inviting their own parents to their home or to spend time with their children because they did not have to worry about what their parents would think of them and how they "kept" their houses or raised their children. Others assumed that their in-laws would understand a woman's tendency to want to see her own parents. Thus, the expectation that daughters will stay close to their parents following marriage becomes a self-fulfilling prophecy. As a result, men tend to get "pulled into" their wives' families following marriage while women are not pulled into their husbands' families. Mothers of sons though said they wished things were more equal and that they often felt they were on the outside of their sons' lives looking in on them.

What happens though when both spouses are male or both spouses are female? Will sons still pull back from their families of origin following marriage to focus on the provider role when they have a husband? Will daughters try to pull their wives into their families of orientation as do heterosexual women or will their wife's need to spend time with *her* parents prevent this? Likewise, how will the conflict that sometimes ensued following the child's "coming out of the closet" earlier in life affect relationships with parents once the child marries? These and other questions will be answered in this chapter.

There is likely to be some variation in the effect of marriage on intergenerational relationships when children enter into a same-sex marriage. As we saw in chapter 2, disclosure of the child's sexual orientation (or "coming out") results in greater ambiguity in those relationships. It results in negative as well as positive emotions between the parent and adult child. A homosexual marriage may heighten that ambiguity and result in greater conflict. Likewise, marriage brings the relationship into the public arena, thus leading to anxiety for those parents who have not redefined their ideas of what it means to be gay/lesbian or who have not accepted their child's sexual orientation. These parents may not have yet told family or friends about their child's homosexuality. Thus, it is expected that relationships between parents and adult children will worsen overall following marriage to a greater extent for lesbian and gay children than for straight children. There may be less effect though for those parents who have fully accepted their child's sexual orientation.

Likewise, if same-sex unions are indeed changing the nature of marriage, then the gender differences for married sons versus married daughters will not replicate those found in heterosexual couples. Same-sex couples are free to rewrite the rules of marriage anew and not fall back on traditional definitions of the husband's role versus the wife's role. If homosexual couples are in fact transforming marriage, they may also change the impact of marriage on their relationships with other family members and make them more equal. As such, same-sex marriage may make marriage a less "greedy" institution.

THE EFFECT OF MARRIAGE

The marriage itself has an important impact on the parent–adult child relationship for lesbian and gay adult children. For some, like the daughter discussed in the previous chapter, it was the permanence of the relationship and all that comes from marriage being a legally recognized institution that made a difference to her parents. The ability to marry put the union into a known and accepted context. That is, their child's relationship was legitimized and normalized by the institution of marriage. The presence of others at the wedding and having a religious official preside over it also made it clear that the marriage was affirmed by friends and other family members as well and that it was sanctioned by their faith. For example, one daughter said,

> I think that the marriage itself [meant] a big deal to my mother. For us, we did it more for financial and security reasons. It was our [earlier] commitment ceremony that was important to us. But for my mom, it made a big difference, maybe because she is Catholic, and we had a priest presiding. All of my Catholic family were there, and it was, or must have been, okay with them. You are supposed to be legally married in Catholicism. . . . So there was a change in her after that. It is funny. She always sends us a card on the date of that anniversary, whereas we celebrate on the date of our commitment ceremony.

Another mother said that it was during her son's wedding and reception that she saw the extent of her son-in-law's love for her son. His willingness to include their family in the planning of the ceremony and the ceremony itself made her appreciate her son-in-law even more than she had previously. Likewise, many of the parents could see that their new child-in-law was no different from their own child and had an equally "good background" when they met his or her family. One father said, "I could see that she [meaning his new daughter-in-law] had a really solid extended family, and so I just felt better about her and the relationship after that . . . I would not want her parents to think less of my daughter, so you have to be open to their daughter too."

Parents are also relieved when their child finds a lifelong partner, given that the pool of eligible same-sex partners is smaller than the pool of eligible heterosexuals. One father said, "Since my daughter first came out, I was worried that she was not going to be able to find someone. It was easier for her brother to find someone, a given. I was just worried that she would always have to be alone, so I was elated when she said that she was getting married."

The fact that parents now had to "go public" with their child's relationship or come out of the family closet also changed the relationship. Parents were resentful of their children when they first announced their intention to marry because now they had to tell others—those to whom they had not yet disclosed their child's sexual orientation—that their child was gay or lesbian. The fact that it was no longer a secret and that they did not have to risk embarrassment anymore provided great relief after the ceremony though. One mother said, "Okay, it was all out in the open and nothing bad had happened. . . . The grandparents were all okay with it. . . . We even seemed to *gain* some clients when word got around. Her parents were normal. It was all normal." Parents also became more defensive of their children when they had to publicize the wedding. Nancy, one of the lesbian daughters, said that it was when her mother Arlene was inviting extended family to the wedding that she became such an advocate of gay and lesbian rights. One of Arlene's uncles said he was opposed to same-sex marriage because the Bible clearly stated that only people of the opposite sex should form a union. Arlene, who originally opposed her daughter's disclosure of lesbianism, responded by arguing for Nancy's *right* to marry like everyone else and pointed out the places in the Bible that contradicted the uncle's assumption. As such, Arlene went from being a critic to an *advocate* when knowledge of the wedding went public. This may have been the result of her gaining more information herself about homosexuality as well as wanting to protect her daughter against other people's discrimination.

Thus, part of the change in the parent–adult child bond occurs because marriage makes the child's union more "normal." Parents were more likely to see the relationship as falling within the boundaries of what is considered acceptable in our society, which increased their own acceptance. Their greater ease was palpable in their relationship with their child and with his or her spouse as well. One child said that her mother told her she felt more comfortable visiting when she and her lover were no longer "just living together." Marriage not only made the relationship more respectable but also made their children's homes more accessible to parents as a result.

The *heterosexual* children's actual marriage made a difference to the parent–adult child relationship as well, in at least some cases. However, the differences were not quite as stark because marriage was always expected for heterosexual children and going public with the relationship was usually not a concern for parents. Marriage made the greatest difference when parents were critical of their adult child living together with a partner. Parents were relieved when their child decided to get married, which then improved their relationship. One of the daughters said,

> Both of my parents were so upset about our living together. They saw it as living in sin. They were upset with both me and [my husband]. For a while they wouldn't even talk to me. I think they assumed it was [husband's name], as the guy, who didn't want to get married. So they were mad at him too. Then, as soon as we announced that we were getting married, it was all water under the bridge. . . . Actually being married is just more important to them.

Only one of the parents of a *heterosexual* child was concerned about going public with her child's pending wedding. This mother believed that her future daughter-in-law's social class and educational level were below that of her own family's and that their marriage was degrading to both her son and the family's overall social standing. For months the mother refused to discuss the wedding or tell extended family about her son's fiancée. Family members were eventually notified of the wedding with invitations. The mother chose to help with planning the wedding only when it became clear that family and her own friends were going to attend. The wedding itself and the process of going public did not improve her relationship with either her son or her daughter-in-law though, as she continued to discriminate against her daughter-in-law. In fact, she discriminated against her grandchildren from this marriage as well, according to the daughter-in-law.[6]

Thus, marriage can improve parent-child relationships when children are heterosexual as well as homosexual due to the importance of marriage and its meaning to society. It is less of an issue when children are heterosexual though because parents can assume that their children will eventually marry and that it is only a matter of time. Marriage has a greater effect when children are homosexual because it also connotes an acceptance by society and family and friends. Going public is also less of a concern when children are heterosexual because their marriage partners are much more likely to be acceptable to parents and perceived others. Heterosexual partners are less likely to fall outside of a parent's range of satisfactory spouses for their child.

The social construction of the gender of the marital partner also affects the relationship between the couple and their parents. In this regard, it makes a big difference whether your child is heterosexual or homosexual in how his or her marriage affects the parent-child relationship. In heterosexual marriages, mothers sometimes felt they had "lost" their son following marriage, whether because of conflict with the daughter-in-law or because her son was spending his leisure time with his wife and children or his wife's family. Husbands indeed said that, to some extent, they took a step back from their extended families to focus on their careers and providing for their own family. Wives pull their husbands into their own families because of their expected continued closeness with their parents. Thus, marriage for heterosexual sons can leave parents feeling on the outside of their sons' lives. For example, one of the mothers said,

> We never see my son anymore—since he got married. He and his wife spend all of their time with her family. . . . I think that his wife does not like us, and I really don't know why. I have asked my son why they don't visit more, and he says that it is just that his wife is shy . . . so I tell him that we really miss him and want to see him more. . . . Sometimes months will go by, and we don't hear from him.

Gay sons though said they felt less conflicted between spending time with their spouse and their parents. Rod, for example, stated,

> I probably spend more time with my mother than any of my siblings. My sisters are busy with their kids, even though they live closer [to my mother]. Plus, they have husbands. I mean, I have a husband too, but Robert does not expect me to cater to him or him to me. We can both do things for ourselves. My sisters' husbands though do less for themselves. . . . My brother, well, he lives closer [to my mother] too. I think that she [my sister-in-law] and my mother get along fine, but I think that my brother still feels that his place is with her [rather than my mother]. . . . There is just less competition between Rob and my mother than between my mother and sister-in-law.

Likewise, one of the mothers said,

> When I go to visit my son and his spouse, I feel like I am visiting my two sons. . . . Like when I am there, I can do for them, without offending them—cook breakfast, clean up. . . . I don't feel like I am intruding on someone else's home. . . . My daughter-in-law is wonderful and has never made me feel like I am stepping on her toes, but I would not assume as much in her house.

Thus, the social construction of heterosexual marriage and the accompanying traditional wife and husband roles account for some of the tension that mothers, in particular, experience following their heterosexual child's marriage. Competition arises between the mother and child's spouse because traditional marriage includes a division of labor where husbands and wives are dependent on one another. Husbands and wives cannot leave their spouses for long periods of time because of a gendered specialization of labor. Likewise, mothers' and daughters-in-law's central roles in creating family put them in competition for the husband's time and attention. Those same gender expectations allow for parents and gay sons to continue their relationships with little change following marriage. Men's expected independence allows for their husbands to leave in order to visit parents, from short to extended stays away from home. Likewise, parents feel more comfortable visiting the home of two men, versus a husband and wife, since the running of the home continues to be more of a wife's domain. Mothers feel less free to settle into the home of another woman though. Wives also have greater responsibilities to the home than do husbands in heterosexual marriages, sometimes making it harder for them to travel alone in order to visit a parent. Thus, it is the way we think of both heterosexual marriage and gender roles that allows gay men to have better relationships with their parents following marriage. In addition, the gay men in this study did not have children while the heterosexual men did, also adding a competing demand on their time that took from their attention to parents. Sam explained, "Kris really does not mind when I go to see my mother. I mean, he can take care of himself while I am gone. . . . I mean he misses me, but it is not expected that I am going to stay home and take care of him the way that my sister takes care of my brother-in-law." Likewise, Kim said, "I am the one who takes care of my mom, and [my wife] doesn't mind. It is assumed that if you are a woman who does not have a *husband* that you will take care of your parents. [My wife] is less needy of me than my brothers-in-law [are of my sisters]."

To some extent, this also suggests then that homosexual marriage offers a clean slate in which the roles of each spouse can be defined anew, rather than replicating the prevailing institution of heterosexual marriage and its gendered division of labor. The roles of husband and wife have not been reproduced for the two men or the two women. Instead, the gender roles still present in heterosexual marriage are being dismantled in same-sex marriage. This then may change marriage and our assumptions about it. Marriage no longer has to be the greedy institution that holds adults back from participating in the wider community or with extended family.[7] The remainder of this book will look at other ways in which same-sex marriage is redefining what we mean by marriage and providing a clean slate on which couples can redefine their roles more consistently with twenty-first-century values.

Parents-in-law tend to have better relationships with their lesbian daughters-in-law than their heterosexual sons-in-law. This is because of the work and skills that women often assume in a family to stay in contact and to nurture relationships, such as reaching out to one's in-laws. Samantha explained, "Well, I think that Aimee just tries harder to get to know them [my parents] and to keep in touch. She sends them letters and e-mails them. My brother-in-law doesn't do any of that. . . . I think that family relationships are just more important to women than to men. They want to be connected to family, even if it is their spouse's family. Thus, parents feel more comfortable with a daughter-in-law than a son-in-law because of the expectation that women are closer to parents than men are and what we think of as feminine. In contrast, sons-in-law, like sons, are assumed to be more independent and aloof.

One mother also pointed out that she has more in common with her lesbian daughter's wife than with her other daughter's husband. She elaborated, "Well, we have more similar tastes—in movies, in hobbies. There is just more for me to talk about [with Shannon's wife than her other daughter's husband]. I am also just more comfortable with her style, with another woman than with a man. . . . We have the same way of interacting and the same perspective, I guess."

Mothers often feel greater competition with their son's wife than with their daughter's wife. This may be due to the expectation in our society of mothers-in-law being in conflict with their son's wives, exemplified in the media with recent films such as *Monster-in-Law* and television programs such as *Everybody Loves Raymond*. However, it may also be due to the phenomena of men being pulled into their wives' families following heterosexual marriage, which does not appear to be happening with same-sex marriage.[8] Lesbian couples were much more likely to spend equal amounts of time with both sets of parents, assuming all else was equal, or for each of the women to spend more time alone with her own parents. In contrast, heterosexual couples spent more time with the wife's family when all else was equal.[9] One of the heterosexual daughters explained,

> We spend more time with my family, yes. It is not that we don't get along with his family or that we don't spend some time with them, but no, I would not say that it is equal. . . . I think that they [the in-laws] understand that a woman needs to see more of her parents than a man is expected to do. . . . As long as they get

to see *enough* of us and the kids too, which they do. . . . I mean my sister-in-law spends more time with my in-laws than her in-laws too.

Same-sex marriage can also have a negative impact on the parent-and-child bond though. Some of the children realized just how embarrassed their parents were by their sexuality and how differently their parents were handling their weddings versus their heterosexual siblings' weddings. One daughter elaborated,

> When my sister got married, my parents invited all of the family friends and my father's work associates. There was a much shorter [guest] list for my wedding though. *None* of my father's work associates were invited and only a few family friends. I realized that it was because my parents were embarrassed. . . . They did not want everyone to realize that their daughter was a lesbian. It really hurt. . . . It wasn't so much that they spent less money on my wedding than my sister's [wedding] that bothered me as much as the fact that it was just less of a celebratory occasion for them. It was like they were just going through the motions for me rather than being happy about it.

Other children said that their parents' first reaction when they declared they were getting married was to shout out "No!" or to otherwise reveal their unhappiness over the marriage or the wedding ceremony itself. One mother said, "No! Please! Just wait until I die." Some parents were horrified that the wedding ceremony was going to make the relationship more public. Others realized that the marriage might introduce new situations in their child's homosexual lifestyle to which they would have to adjust, such as having or adopting children. In addition, they realized that their child's partner was now going to be a son-in-law/daughter-in-law and that the relationship would be permanent. Each of these things was a challenge to the parent that made it harder to be in favor of their child's marriage. Children, sometimes surprised by their parents' reactions, realized that their parents were somewhat homophobic or at least not 100 percent supportive of their relationships. Either situation complicated the parent-child bond and added greater conflict and ambiguity to it.

Parents are often mournful when their child marries because they can no longer hope that their child's sexuality is a "phase" that they will outgrow. Connie said that her husband has always attributed their son's sexuality to being a "stage" that would change. She said, "He told me that he would outgrow it just like he outgrew the spiked hair and grunge clothes. But ten years after coming out, he got married. *He* [the husband] still ignored it [that is, did not acknowledge the marriage], but I could not do that."

Thus, not all of the parents and their children reconcile as a result of marriage. While many of the relationships that were mediocre got better, as was described earlier in the chapter, the most estranged relationships stayed the same. Kris's parents, for example, continued to blame Sam for "making Kris gay," which was how they rationalized Kris's sexuality. Likewise, parents who pretended that their child was heterosexual or who never spoke of the obvious nature of the relationship continued to turn a blind eye to the reality. These parents had not been invited to what were usually small marriage ceremonies with a justice of the peace or at the local courthouse. Some of the children said they did not want to "rock the boat" by forcing the issue with their parents. Other children said they wanted to respect their parent's choice not to confront it, or as they put it, "rub their nose in it." As such, these parents continued not to ask questions about the nature of the relationship. Interestingly, some parents reverted occasionally to assuming that their child and his or her spouse were just friends, even though they knew that a wedding ceremony had taken place. For example, one of the lesbian respondents said,

> It was really shocking. . . . One time my in-laws visited and stayed in the guest room. Throughout the whole visit, they treated me like I was just a friend of Susan's. . . . Her mother was helping her to pick out furniture for our new house, and neither one of them consulted me on the matter. I was furious. . . . Then, when they got ready to go, my mother-in-law said to me, "Thank you for letting us use your room while we were here," as if Susan and I slept in separate rooms. I didn't say anything, but I couldn't believe the way that they just ignored the reality. I mean, come on. . . . They did not come to the wedding, but they knew all well and good that we were married. . . . They would not have assumed that their other children did not sleep with their spouses.

WHAT MAKES A DIFFERENCE?

There were several factors that increased the likelihood of parents' accepting their child's same-sex marriage and not being embarrassed by the prospect of its public nature. Such parents were more likely to have children who came out of the closet to them earlier in life, usually as teenagers or as young adults. In contrast, Samantha came out of the closet at the same time that she announced her decision to marry, giving her parents no time to get used to her being a lesbian before getting used to the idea of her same-sex marriage. Parents who are more accepting also tend to be more educated and liberal. When one of the women came out to her father, he said (although it was not his first comment), "Well, at least you are not a Republican. That would have been worse." Moreover, parents who are more positive about their child's same-sex marriage tend to have friends and family members who make complimentary remarks about the couple. One of the daughters said, "By the time that I got married [or at least announced her intention to do so], my mother had already told a bunch of people, first family and then friends, that we were a couple, and they all said how great that was and how happy they were for me. That made a big difference to my mom."

Parents are also less likely to be embarrassed by their child's sexuality and marriage if they can separate out their feelings about homosexuality from the relationship. Those who made this comment said they had to set aside any homophobic thoughts they had from the couple and their decision to marry. One mother said,

> I am from a different generation. This [homosexuality] was not common when I was growing up. The Catholic Church and the nuns told us that it was a sin. . . . I did not want to think about my daughter committing a sin . . . or her partner being responsible for that . . . so I had to set it all aside and just be happy for them. I had to think about the fact that my child was getting married and not the *type* of marriage that it was.

Finally, parents who are more accepting of their child's marriage tend to be the same parents who describe their child's earlier years as troubled due to their sexuality. This included mothers whose sons had been beaten up by classmates for not "fitting in" or whose daughters had despaired because they were "different" and had refused to go to school dances. These earlier troubles not only made such parents closer to their children when they were young but also made them more appreciative when their child did find a mate.

In sum, it was assumed that same-sex marriage would have a predominantly negative effect on parent–adult child relationships. It was expected that this would result due to same-sex marriage being outside of what is considered "normal" or expected, causing parents to be ambivalent at best about their child's marriage. Marriage would make visible what might have been a family secret and raise new issues for parents, such as how to relate to their new child-in-law. In addition, marriage cements the relationship and prevents any hope that the child will revert to a heterosexual marriage. Certainly, for some parent-child bonds, the child's same-sex marriage does make the relationship worse. Parents were estranged from their children due to their rejection of their sexuality. More often than not though, parents came around to accept their child's sexual orientation. For these parents and their children, same-sex marriage actually *improved* relationships rather than undermining them. This improvement in the relationship though is in direct contrast to the way in which parent-and-child relationships sometimes worsened when sons entered into heterosexual marriages. Heterosexual sons sometimes felt they had to step back from their relationships with their parents in order to concentrate on their own families, while lesbian and gay children did not.

Thus, same-sex marriage alters relationships between parents and homosexual children as it does for parents and heterosexual children, but it does so in different ways. For those parents who are able to set aside their feelings about homosexuality, marriage can actually improve relationships between parents and adult children. Relationships with married gay sons are not as detrimentally affected by marriage relative to married heterosexual sons due to the way that we think of traditional heterosexual marriage and marital roles. Gay sons feel greater freedom to visit with parents relative to heterosexual sons, who follow the traditional script of a husband's place being with his wife and in his own home. This script emphasizes a husband and wife's dependence on one another and a sexual division of labor where men and women have different responsibilities. Gay sons are also freer to visit parents than daughters/sisters who are expected to keep the home and care for their husbands and children. Likewise, parents feel closer to their lesbian daughters-in-law than to their heterosexual sons-in-law because of women's tendency to reach out more to family and parents' expectations that daughters will be closer than sons (and thus, daughters-in-law than sons-in-law). To some extent then, homosexual marriage is challenging the conventions of heterosexual marriage and is allowing couples to define their own roles on a blank slate. However, those roles continue to be influenced by gender expectations, suggesting the overpowering significance of definitions of masculinity versus femininity in our society. This does not negate the fact that same-sex marriage is creating new meanings of marriage and challenging the traditional expectations of heterosexual marriage as a result.

Many feminists, who would like to see marriage become more egalitarian, have certainly hoped for such a change. At a time in which so many mothers of young children work outside of the home, many would like to see men and women jointly share labor in the home as well as power and decision making in marriage. They would also like to see marriage become a less greedy institution that prevents spouses from maintaining connections to extended families and the community. Same-sex marriages may become the role models for this to happen since gay men and lesbians are more likely to maintain close ties with parents following marriage. In addition, as will be shown in the next chapter, same-sex couples are more likely to spend time together and have joint interests. Marriage advocates would like to see heterosexual marriages change in this direction as well. There is important evidence for the extent to which husbands and wives increasingly live separate lives with little time spent together or in joint activities.[10] However, it is argued here that marriages more similar to same-sex marriages, in terms of having joint interests, spending time together, and being more egalitarian, would be more fulfilling for both women and men.

In the next chapter, we will look at why gay and lesbian couples choose to marry during a time in which there are so many available options for adult living arrangements and the likelihood of divorce is so high. It will also consider how the reasons for marrying differ for homosexual versus heterosexual individuals and the implications of this. This discussion will shed further light on the changing nature of marriage in the twenty-first century. It will also help parents to understand the nature of their child's same-sex marriage.

Chapter 5

Reasons for Marrying and the Division of Labor in the Home

In recent years, there has been a record number of Americans who have never married.[1] Decreasing rates of marriage are found particularly among younger Americans. In fact, one in four of today's adults between the ages of twenty-five and thirty-four may never marry. Only about half of never-married individuals say they would like to marry eventually. Caucasians are more likely to marry than racial minorities with blacks being the least likely to marry. Men are more likely to remain unmarried than women.[2] Why some adults continue to choose to marry during a time in which the divorce rate remains high, marriage rates are low, and numerous alternative options to marriage are socially sanctioned baffles today's family sociologists.

Changes in the economy since the recession of 2006 may explain why some Americans choose not to marry. More women cite the importance of finding a spouse with a steady job in looking for a potential spouse than any other given factor, such as having at least as much education or having the same religious or ethnic background. In fact, the pool of employed, young men (twenty-five to thirty-four years of age) has shrunk steadily from 1990 to 2012.[3] Marriage has thus become a capstone in an adult person's life or a symbol that the person has achieved other statuses (being employed, stable, and perhaps even owning a home or having children) that convey adulthood. Marriage is also symbolic in that it is a way of elevating the relationship above all others and a way of "bragging" about the quality of the relationship and its likelihood of enduring. Despite socially sanctioned alternatives, such as living together, the strength of the marriage ethic is strong enough in our society that people continue to marry serially for shorter periods of time, a process referred to as the "marriage-go-round."[4] In fact, older adults who are not married are stigmatized and pitied. They state that family, friends, and colleagues make their "singlism" highly visible, often in unintentional ways.[5] Marriage is also "more than [just] being together."[6] Its distinctive lifestyle encourages people to give up the self-interested ways of an unattached single and instead to commit to the obligations of a spouse. Married individuals will forego risky lifestyles and choices knowing that others depend on them. This is a healthier way of life that benefits married individuals in numerous ways.[7]

In a study of the Netherlands, where same-sex marriage has been legal since 2001, gay and lesbian couples gave reasons for marriage that were very similar to those of heterosexuals. Among the top reasons given, couples stated that they married to express a commitment to the relationship and an intention to stay together, both to each other and to their families and friends. They also wanted to ensure the well-being of children, cement the bond at a time that was meaningful in the relationship, and make a political statement about the equality of gay men and lesbians.[8] Finally, they wished to establish a legal bond that would allow for the benefits of a joint economic life.

An earlier study in the United States found that homosexuals' attitudes about marriage are also very similar to the attitudes of heterosexuals. For example, the percentages who believe that divorce is best if you cannot work out problems or that the rewards of being a parent are worth the cost and work are quite similar for homosexuals and heterosexuals. However, lesbians and gay men are significantly *less* likely than heterosexual women and men, respectively, to agree that it is better to be married than single. They are also less likely to believe that young people should not live together unless they are married.[9] Thus, although similar, lesbian and gay men are somewhat more skeptical about the benefits of marriage and are more open to cohabitation. However, this study was done in 2002, at a time in which same-sex marriage was not legal in the United States and thus not even within the realm of possibility for gay men and lesbians to consider for themselves.

This chapter investigates the reasons that married homosexuals give for marrying. Results will shed light on how the homosexual community views marriage and whether or not same-sex marriage is changing the meaning of marriage in America. Findings will also help us to understand why couples choose to marry at a time in which there are so many alternatives to marriage and divorce. In fact, marriage rates in Massachusetts for the overall population declined steadily during the time in which these couples took their vows, from 6.5 in 2004 to 5.5 in 2011 per 1,000 population.[10] Understanding why gay men and lesbians wish to marry will also assist parents in understanding the contours of same-sex marriage.

WHY MARRY?

There are two categories of reasons that lesbians and gay men wish to marry: political and nonpolitical reasons. The political motivations include furthering GLBT rights and reforming marriage. Nonpolitical reasons are ones that are similar to those that heterosexuals give for wanting to marry. Some lesbians and gay men give reasons that are solely either political or nonpolitical while others have multiple reasons for marrying that cross both categories.

Political Reasons

Many of the men and women saw marrying as a vehicle for furthering GLBT rights. These political reasons were given not only by well-educated and younger individuals but also by a broad cross section of the men and women. The most common reason that was given is that marriage allows individuals to exercise their equal rights. One woman in her fifties said,

> I have waited my whole life for this, and I wasn't sure if it would ever come. . . . Marriage is a right that all adults should have access to. Why should any man and woman have the right to marry, and not me and my partner? . . . Other couples can make medical decisions for one another, share insurance, declare their love for one another. We should have the same rights. . . . I have picketed for this right. I have walked around neighborhoods with petitions and volunteered for [political] candidates who support gay rights. . . . I hope that it will be the start of gaining other rights too and let people see that we are not that different [from them].

Indeed, since declaring the Defense of Marriage Act unconstitutional in 2013, marriage now confers federal rights to same-sex couples including Social Security survivor benefits and Supplemental Security Income (SSI) and disability spousal benefits; joint parenting rights and custodial rights to children and shared property; family visitation rights (in hospitals and prisons) and next-of-kin status; legal status regarding stepchildren; federal and state income tax deductions, credits, and rates exemptions; immigration rights; and assistance and rights to family members of deployed military servants. Prior to this though, same-sex couples were denied the basic financial and legal rights of a partner.

Others said that same-sex marriage made the numbers of gay and lesbian couples more visible. Likewise, they stated that being married gave them the right to kiss and to act like a couple in public. That is, it makes homosexuality more accepted. One woman explained,

> One of the best things about getting married was that we could kiss during the ceremony, in front of everyone else, without being self-conscious. . . . When you are gay or a lesbian you are constantly aware of how much people stare at you. You are always self-conscious. [Laughing,] but we got to kiss in public without caring if we were being judged or not.

A few of the respondents said more simply that marriage allows them to make their relationship known to colleagues and acquaintances to whom they have previously not confided.

In relation to the above reasons, men and women said that they married to let other people know that they are just like them, that is, that they too share a life and home with someone and that they intend to spend the rest of their lives together. One man said, "I want other people to know that this is *my* equivalent of their husband, or their wife. I want them to know that we love one another just like they love their spouse." Later he added, "People think that gay men are out screwing everything that moves, but we are not all like that. I want people to see that we settled down and bought a house just like they did. We are a respectable family just like they are."

The final political reason to marry is to show how marriage can be, or to make marriage less traditional and more egalitarian. Well-educated lesbians are more likely to give this answer. Jackie explained,

> I see my sisters married, and while I love my brothers-in-law, things are not fair in their marriages. My sisters do much more of the housework and care of the children. Their careers always come second to their husbands' careers. . . . Lesbians can be the role models for how to do things fairly and equally. We share the housework. It is not any more my responsibility than Linda's. We encourage each other's careers and don't prioritize one person's over another's. We make decisions together. There isn't one person who is head [of the couple]. I hope that other women will see that and at least see an option for how marriage can be.

Nonpolitical Reasons

Gay men and lesbians also gave nonpolitical reasons for marrying that were closely aligned with the reasons that heterosexuals gave. Similar to heterosexual couples, many of the women said that marriage was the best environment to raise children. Consider the following comment given by one of the lesbians:

> We knew that we wanted to have kids, and I think that the best place to raise kids is to be married. I mean, we had already had a commitment ceremony, and

I knew that I could trust [name] to always stay together. Once marriage became an option though, we decided that we could make that permanence legal *and* share legal rights to the children we adopted. . . . Plus, it is expensive to have children, and it is nice to have the tax benefits to marrying too, when you have to buy new sneakers every six months and soccer uniforms.

Siobhan, for example, wants the legal protections that come with marriage, particularly if she has children. She said, "If we have kids and one of us goes out of the country for work or something, that person needs to be a legal parent to come and go with the child. . . . If we get a divorce, each person needs legal protection and rights of access to the child. . . . If one of us dies, the other spouse should get every possible benefit to keep the family going." Likewise, Kim explained, "Marriage connotes stability, which is the best thing in raising children. We really wanted to get married and to become members of a church community so that we could instill those values of stability and good morals for our child."

Both lesbians and gay men stated that they decided to marry because it was the next step in their relationship. Kris explained, "We had been together for a year and a half and had bought a house together. . . . We had lived together, what, a year at that point? I knew that this was the person that I wanted to be with for the rest of my life. I was in love, and I wanted Sam to know just how much I loved him. . . . It was the right time, so I asked him to be my husband." Others said they married to let their family and friends know that their relationship had reached the level of marriage, versus it being a declaration to one another. Phil said, "I had told my parents that George and I were permanently together, that this was for good. But I could tell that they were still uncertain, especially my father who did not see us together that much. So I figured that if we got married that they would really get it and know that . . . our relationship had reached that level of forever."

Similar to heterosexuals, men and women said they married to declare the relationship permanent. Marriage is believed to be the best way of guaranteeing an enduring relationship, whether because it is legally binding or a public declaration. It lessens the fear of abandonment and increases the likelihood that its members will specialize in a division of labor. Gay men and women, however, tend not to specialize the tasks of marriage. Instead, they want the security of a lifelong relationship and the opportunity to increase the likelihood of that permanence.

In summary, many lesbians and gay men choose to marry in order to exercise their rights and to show they are like every other couple. That is, they attempt to make "normal" their homosexual relationships. Some have even participated in the political process to guarantee those rights. Older couples have waited a long time to exercise such entitlements. In addition to financial gains in the tax code, marriage guarantees legal rights surrounding children, inheritance, and receipt of federal benefits. Gay men and lesbians want their relationships and sexual orientation to be more visible and to feel comfortable as a couple in public. Homosexual couples also wish to marry for reasons that are similar to heterosexuals. They see marriage as an enforceable trust that increases the likelihood of permanence, an optimal environment to raise children, a declaration of the importance of the relationship, and the logical next step in the union.

The fact that many couples will eventually marry during a time in which there are many alternative adult living arrangements and while the likelihood of divorce is still high suggests the continued preference for marriage over remaining single. Slightly over half of never-married individuals would like to marry eventually.[11] Indeed, the very fact that the GLBT community and its supporters have fought so hard for the right to marry suggests the continued importance of the institution. Marriage is expected to increase the likelihood of a couple staying together because of its public declaration and legal status. Couples will be more willing to work out their problems when it is harder to separate. They are also more likely to invest in the relationship and to treat one another with an expectation of staying together permanently. Married couples will make fewer risky decisions and live more stable lives when they know that someone else depends on them. As a result, marriage is a "transformative" experience that changes people's lives in a way in which others wish to participate. Marriage improves the relationship because people have this trust and thus invest more in the relationship. As such, marriage is expected to provide greater fulfillment than other adult living arrangements and relationships. It is what elevates this relationship as the most important one in an adult person's life. The right to marry then has been an important victory for the homosexual community.

Gay men and lesbian women point out though that they are not looking for a replication of heterosexual marriage. Although they want to obtain many of the rights and privileges that correspond with marriage, they also wish to create marriages that differ from those of heterosexual couples. Gay men and lesbians prefer egalitarian marriages that optimize benefits for both spouses and in which they equally share family roles and decision-making power. For this reason, the next section will investigate how individuals in same-sex marriages share the division of labor in the home.

THE DIVISION OF LABOR IN THE HOME

Who in a marriage is going to take responsibility for housework and the rearing of children has been a source of contention in heterosexual marriages since the 1960s and 1970s. Although vast numbers of women have returned to the workforce full time since the 1960s, changes in the home have not occurred to balance that shift. Women continue to take responsibility for the "second shift" at home to the point of working an extra month per year in comparison to men. Likewise, childcare while both parents work continues to be the responsibility of the couple rather than the American government stepping up to provide subsidized, guaranteed, and regulated care to help families. These issues became the rallying cry of the women's liberation movement beginning in the 1960s and the focus of feminist reformers. It also became a source of contention in individual marriages. Despite some recent change, who does what in the home continues to be an important issue today.

Strides have been made in the division of labor in the home. However, this is not uniform across all couples and in most cases is still not equal. The place in which men have made the greatest contribution is in the area of childcare. Fathers have tripled the amount of time that they spend with children since 1965. Thus, men's greater involvement is in the area that is most central to the functions of a family, raising children. Women still perform more of the work in the home while men work more hours outside of the home, arguably to the benefit of men's careers and the detriment of women's careers. Overall, women put in five more hours of work per week in paid and unpaid work than men.[12] This disparity also affects the amount of leisure and sleep to which women have access.

The same-sex couples in this study were more likely to share home labor, including childcare, housework, cooking, and laundry, than the heterosexual couples. First of all, there was less "specialization" (or a division with one person being responsible for the home and children while the other person worked outside of the home) in same-sex couples. In only one lesbian household did one of the women stay home with the children while the other woman was the sole breadwinner. Such a division of labor was more common among families with children under eighteen years of age in the heterosexual families, although it was still a minority of families. In other heterosexual families, both partners worked outside of the home with a few wives working only part time. This is consistent with research in both the United States and the Netherlands that found that homosexual couples tend not to assign roles of breadwinner versus homemaker and that same-sex couples are more egalitarian in sharing housework.[13] This book will also examine couples' reasons for dividing labor equally and *how* they go about dividing it.

Both gay men and lesbians stated that they shared household labor and child-rearing equally out of (1) a sense of fairness and equity and (2) because they wished to spend the time together. They said they prefer to do most things together in order to be with one another. This then results in a shared division of labor. For example, couples often cooked together to have time to talk to one another at the end of each day. It was then that they could share the events of the day before children arrived for the evening meal. Even in families where one person preferred to take responsibility for the task, the other person would help and lighten the overall amount of work. The fact that they were sharing in the cooking also made it a less onerous duty. Several of the couples said that they looked forward to this time together every day.

Gay men and lesbians took into account one another's preferences in dividing labor. Again though, they attempted to make housework an opportunity to share time. Charlotte and Natalia divided their meal preparation with one person doing the baking and the other doing the cooking on the stove. This meant they were both together in the kitchen at the same time and each was doing what they most enjoyed in meal preparation. Rod said he did most of the indoor housework while his husband did the yard work and gardening. Rod said his husband loved working outside while he did not. Usually they set part of Saturday aside to do this and would take breaks together while they did so.

There was no assumption that one person would be automatically responsible for certain things, unlike heterosexual households where couples tended to fall back on a gendered division of labor. In this manner, couples were trying to be fair to one another and create an egalitarian marriage. Even Barb, who was the sole breadwinner, and Marie, who stayed at home with the children, shared the work that was done around the house in the evenings and on weekends. They also equally shared decision making and responsibility for their children. In a traditional heterosexual marriage though, decision making is sometimes tied to the principal breadwinner. In contrast, homosexual couples prioritize equity and equality.

Couples tended to tackle things they were unsure of together. For lesbian couples, this sometimes included fixing things around the house and heavy yard work. Charlotte said,

> We had *no* idea of how to get a vegetable garden started, so we took a class together. . . . We set some time aside in the spring and went out and rented a rototiller together. We had a nursery deliver the topsoil, and we took turns running the rototiller to mix the old and new soils. I would not call it fun, and we

were both exhausted at the end. . . . But we were proud that we figured it all out together and without too much help.

Likewise Siobhan added, "It was a given that neither one of us knew how to tackle home projects. . . . After we bought our house, my dad came to help us get started. Then we would do it together. If one of us forgot what he said or how to do something, usually the other one would remember. Or one of us anyway would be able to figure it out."

Couples tried to create equity and equality in other ways as well. When both spouses preferred not to do a certain task, one person would take responsibility and the other would take on another undesirable, and usually related, task. For example, neither Barb nor Marie liked outdoor work. Barb was in better physical shape though, so she volunteered to mow the lawn in the summer. To maintain equity and spend time together, Marie would take responsibility for cleaning yard debris and weeding while Barb mowed. Likewise, Kris and Sam cleaned the bathroom together, but one person would clean the toilet while the other cleaned the shower. Then, the next month they would switch roles. This resulted in a fair division of labor according to both Kris and Sam.

It is not always optimal for both spouses to participate in a task. Natalia said that sometimes she or her partner would bring work home in the evening. At those times, the other spouse would take full responsibility for meal preparation or cleanup. However, both persons had the option of doing this, and both had at some point taken advantage of it. For all couples, each person was capable of fulfilling the other person's responsibilities, although they may have believed that one was better than the other at certain tasks. In contrast, heterosexual couples often divided labor according to traditional gender roles. In these marriages, men often did not cook and had fewer childcare responsibilities while wives did less of the heavy yard work.

In sum, same-sex couples tend to divide labor equally out of a desire for egalitarian relationships and to spend time together. They create equity by doing tasks together, complementing one another's preferred tasks with similar tasks, taking on projects together, and dividing undesirable tasks equitably. Rather than re-creating a traditional division of labor or assigning one person with "pink tasks" and the other with "blue tasks," they have redefined how couples run their households and their families. Same-sex couples create a family life with an eye to equity and equality and spending time together. This is consistent with earlier studies that suggest same-sex couples tend to be more egalitarian and to spend more time together.[14]

Some authors have argued that same-sex marriage may have little impact in changing the institution of marriage because gay men and lesbians have similar attitudes about marriage to heterosexuals.[15] The results presented here though suggest that, at least in Massachusetts, same-sex marriage is, in fact, calling attention to the inequities in traditional marriage and is providing an alternative for how couples might choose to "do marriage." While same-sex couples wish to marry for some of the same reasons as heterosexuals, that is, to provide the optimal place to raise children and to increase the likelihood of permanence, they also wish to make marriage a place that is beneficial for both spouses. Gay men and lesbians stress the importance of equality in marriage and strive to provide equity for both partners. They emphasize spending time together, sharing interests, and building a life that optimizes this unity. Same-sex marriage is thus the role model for how marriage can increase the time overall that couples tend to spend together.[16] Same-sex marriage is not undermining marriage but strengthening it to resist the other social forces that tend to weaken it. As was found in previous chapters, same-sex marriage is not a "greedy" form of marriage that robs each partner of time spent with extended family or in the community, but instead it encourages couples to still participate in those outside interests but to do so together. Same-sex marriage provides a blueprint for how couples might optimally blend their lives together so that they are truly a couple, without detriment to either individual. In same-sex unions, the couple is more than just the sum of each separate life. It is veritably a transformative experience. It is also in direct contrast to traditional heterosexual marriage where one person, often the wife, makes sacrifices for the benefit of the other person's career. This comes through in particular in the division of labor among lesbians and gay men. Same-sex couples divide the labor of the home to optimize both spending time together and creating equity and equality. They share in tasks so that no one person has the bulk of responsibility for household chores or child-rearing. More importantly though, work in the home becomes an opportunity to spend time together, share a life, and build a family. Unequivocally, it is what all couples hope that a married life will provide.

The next chapter will further this line of inquiry by looking at how same-sex couples go about raising a family, if they choose to do so. It will look in particular at the decision to have a child, how couples go about acquiring a child, and then how they go about raising the child. Again, we will look at the process with an eye toward how gay and lesbian couples "do family" or conduct their family life and how that is changing the nature of family in the twenty-first century. It will also help parents to understand the processes that their child may go through if he or she wishes to have children.

Chapter 6

Gay and Lesbian Couples Raising Children

The decision to raise a child and the task of acquiring a child are fundamentally different for same-sex versus heterosexual couples. Same-sex couples must either go through artificial insemination/in vitro fertilization (for lesbians) or surrogacy (for gay men) or choose to adopt a child in order to raise children. In this respect, it requires a conscientious decision and specific effort to add children to the family. Raising children has not always been a part of the gay/lesbian experience. Couples had to keep their homosexuality private in the past due to the extent of homophobia in our society. In contrast, heterosexual couples are *expected* to raise children and can have a child without planning to conceive. Heterosexuality allows couples to reproduce without any other startup costs unless they experience infertility. However, same-sex couples must often pay significant adoption fees or the costs of reproductive technologies if they are not covered by insurance. They enter into the process knowing the financial contribution associated with bringing a child into their family. But the goal of having and raising children for homosexual couples is often the same as that for heterosexual couples—to love and raise a family together. This chapter will examine the process of becoming a parent and how parenting is different for gay and lesbian families versus heterosexual families. It is intended to be a primer for parents to understand the experience of their lesbian or gay children who wish to be parents themselves.

While not all same-sex couples choose to have children, many children are in fact raised by gay or lesbian parents. As of 2013, gay or lesbian couples were raising an estimated two hundred thousand children under the age of eighteen. Of these, thirty thousand children were raised by married same-sex couples. Lesbian, gay, or bisexual individuals who are not part of a couple were raising an estimated minimum 1.2 million children.[1] Forty percent of couples seeking marriage have children living with them already.[2] Some of these children were born during previous heterosexual marriages and thus have a second parent who is heterosexual. Other children, however, are deliberately added to the family by the couple and join them either through adoption or through in vitro fertilization/artificial insemination (for women) and surrogacy (for men).

The costs of either adopting a child or undergoing in vitro fertilization/ artificial insemination (or hiring a surrogate) are relatively expensive for anyone going through this process, heterosexual or homosexual. Lesbian couples have the option of pursuing intrauterine insemination (IUI) where donor sperm is inserted into the uterus of an ovulating woman in the hopes of achieving pregnancy or through in vitro fertilization, where one of the women has her eggs removed following induced ovulation the eggs are implanted with sperm in a laboratory setting, and the eggs are then implanted in the mother's womb. The average cost of in vitro fertilization is twelve thousand dollars but ranges from ten to fifteen thousand.[3] This results in one of the parents having a biological connection to the child. Women who cannot procure sperm from a male friend or family member (perhaps of their partner) must also pay for the cost of the sperm, which is approximately $1,350 to $1,525 per cycle for two vials of sperm, the recommended amount for one cycle. The cost varies by whether or not someone can pick up the sperm from the sperm bank or whether it has to be shipped and how. Thus, the average cost of six months of in vitro fertilization (IVF) is approximately $72,000 if you have available sperm and $80,400 if you do not.[4] This is prohibitively expensive for many couples. Some of these costs might be absorbed by health insurance, and some facilities may offer payment plans or discounts. Ultimately though, the costs may be very high or out of range. Sometimes success can be had on the one or two rounds of IVF or insemination, so costs may not always range as high, at eighty thousand dollars or more. Alternatively, women can consider artificial insemination or IUI, where sperm are implanted in the uterus prior to ovulation. This process produces a success rate as high as 20 percent per cycle.[5] However, this success rate is based on all women, most of whom are experiencing infertility problems or whose husbands have infertility problems. The success rate for lesbian women who require sperm but who do not otherwise have any infertility issues could be higher. In contrast, gay men must pay for the cost of surrogacy, which ranges from $100,000 to $150,000, and which also allows one of the parents to have a biological connection to the child. In some cases, a couple may opt to have a donor egg fertilized with one of the partner's sperm and then implanted into a third person, the carrier, who has no biological connection to the baby. Legal safeguards and contracts come into play, but there are, of course, instances where a surrogate may decide to try to keep the baby herself.

The least expensive option is foster care adoption, which is essentially free. This method of adoption, however, is a lengthy process, rarely includes infants for adoption, and often includes children with disabilities or who are of a different race than their adoptive parents. The adoptive parent is initially a foster parent. However, not all states allow adoption by same-sex couples or individuals known to be in a same-sex relationship. Currently, the following states explicitly deny joint adoption by same-sex couples throughout the state: Kansas, Kentucky, Michigan, Mississippi, Nebraska, North Carolina, Ohio, Utah, and Wisconsin (nine states). In contrast, Arkansas, California, Colorado, Connecticut, Washington, D.C., Illinois, Indiana, Iowa, Maine, Massachusetts, New Jersey, New York, Nevada, Oregon, Vermont, and Washington (sixteen states) do permit joint adoption by same-sex couples. However, social workers may be prejudiced against same-sex adoption and overlook such potential parents, and judges may deny adoption at its final stage. In other states, the laws regarding this are quite ambiguous and vary throughout the state.[6] Private domestic adoptions allow the couple to seek an infant and a caseworker who will be open to same-sex couples adopting, but they cost anywhere from twenty to forty thousand dollars on average. Likewise, international adoptions cost anywhere from eleven to sixty thousand dollars. Most countries that permit international adoption do not *knowingly* allow homosexuals to adopt, although the actual practice allows for it. Those countries that permit their own homosexual citizens to adopt include Belgium, Canada, Denmark, Iceland, the Netherlands, Norway, South Africa, Spain, Sweden, the United Kingdom, and Uruguay.[7]

Most of the research on same-sex couples raising children has looked at the social-psychological implications for children. This is due to the earlier argument that gay and lesbian couples should not be allowed to marry because of concerns about possible negative effects on children. However, the research shows no detrimental effects for children raised in same-sex marriages in terms of school achievement, social adjustment, mental health, gender identity, or sexual orientation. Children raised by lesbian or gay parents do express greater openness or acceptance of homosexuality and bisexuality but are no more likely to grow up to be gay or lesbian themselves. Gay and lesbian parents are also disproportionately white, better educated, and more mature than other families.[8] Thus, same-sex couples can actually benefit their children rather than harming them in terms of the resources they bring to their children and the benefit of becoming parents at an older age. The other topics that were most commonly examined include the transition to adoption and family adaptation and the quality of the relationship between the adoptive parent and child.[9]

This chapter will add to the earlier work by examining additional topics. This will include, among other issues, the initial decision to have a child or not; factors that affect a couple's choice of pathway to parenthood; challenges that arise specific to same-sex couples; and how same-sex couples "do parenting" differently (if at all) from heterosexual couples. Unlike prior research, this chapter considers only those couples that are married or have been married, thus those situations where the family receives the greatest institutional support and where the family structure is closest to the normative two-parent household. Likewise, while earlier research has been mostly from a psychological perspective and focused on outcomes, this chapter will examine parenting in a social context and illustrate the process and social experience of parenting.

THE DECISION TO HAVE A CHILD

According to the results of this study, same-sex couples, particularly gay men, are less likely to parent than heterosexual couples. Nearly all of the heterosexual couples had at least one child. However, none of the gay men who were in their forties or older had a child. The one male couple that was in their thirties wanted to have two or more children, and they planned to pursue adoption in the next year or two. The majority of the lesbian couples had a child or, for the younger women, planned to have a child or adopt. However, there was still a higher percentage of parents among the heterosexual couples than among the lesbian couples. Some of the lesbians also had children from prior heterosexual marriages, but none of the gay men did.

Each individual was asked about the process by which they decided to have a child or not, whether it was a conscious decision, and the factors that they considered in their discussions. All of the gay men and lesbians said they made a conscious decision about whether or not to have a child at some point in the relationship. All of the men, with the exception of the couple that wanted to adopt in a few years, said they started the relationship with no particular inclination either way. With time though, each man came to realize he wanted to spend his time focusing on his career, hobbies, and spouse rather than caring for a child. A typical response for the gay men was as follows:

I like children okay, but not enough that I want to give up working when I want or how much I want. . . . Plus, I enjoy our time with each other and don't want to have to give that up. My sister, she and her husband have to get a *babysitter* to even go out. . . . That is just not for us. . . . At the beginning, when we moved in together . . . and even when we had a commitment ceremony, it was all up in the air; it was an option. After about three or four years, we each independently decided not to adopt though.

All of the male couples said they made their decision through a series of discussions over the course of their relationship. None of the couples engaged in lengthy negotiation since they were almost always in agreement about what they wanted to do. That is, the discussions in the early years of their relationship left the option open. Eventually though, each person came to see that he did not want a child, sometimes realizing that earlier than his partner. None of the men said this led to an argument. However, there was often a time in which one of the men wanted to have a child and the other did not.

A minority of the gay men said they did not intend to have children, not because of career interests or time considerations but because they did not see it as a viable option. One of the men was receiving disability payments due to emotional instability and did not believe having a child was an option for him and his spouse. Another man said he did not want the responsibility of a child and that he was not really family oriented beyond his relationship with his husband. He said he and his partner like to party and have fun. He saw these characteristics as inconsistent with raising children. These two men said they needed only one discussion with their partner about raising a child because the decision was "so obvious."

The lesbian couples that did not plan to have children gave reasons for foregoing parenthood that were similar to the men. Only a small minority of the lesbian women though said they preferred to focus on their careers or "child-free" lifestyles. These women tended to be the most highly educated, with professional jobs, a lifestyle that included weekends away, and extensive interests such as skiing, biking, and photography.

The lesbian couples that either adopted children or had them through fertility treatments (or planned to do so) said they had lengthy discussions with their partners about raising children before their commitment or marriage ceremonies. Usually both spouses from the lesbian couples agreed that they wanted a child, but a few of the women needed to be convinced to have a child. One of the women said her wife was at first opposed to having a child because of the attention that having a child would draw to them and fear that the public would condemn them. This person said it just took time after their commitment ceremony for her partner to become comfortable enough with the reactions of others to agree to adopt. Another woman said her partner just needed the time to do the things she wanted to do before settling down, such as traveling and buying a house. These women described lengthy negotiations in their decision-making process with their spouses. They stated that they did not argue with one another, but they were fearful and emotionally distraught that they might not be able to have a child. They did feel though that their wives took their preferences into consideration in deciding whether or not to have a child.

The vast majority of heterosexual couples either already had a child or intended to have a child within one or two years. The rare heterosexual women who did not have a child said that either they did not want to give up time for themselves or they did not have a child because of financial considerations. These adults stated that they could not afford to do everything they wanted to do, including having children. In particular, they were concerned that they might not be able to have their own home or take vacations if they had children.

Most of the heterosexual adults said that they, along with their spouse, wanted to raise another generation. However, a few of the women said they had to convince their husband to have a child. One of the women said, "He just likes to buy toys for himself . . . motorcycles, snowmobiles, power boats. It took about five years of arguing before he would agree to have one. I [would] like to have a second [child], but he says that I am lucky to have my daughter and not to rock the boat." Heterosexual couples were more likely to argue about having children when they disagreed than were same-sex couples. In addition, heterosexual women were more likely to assume that they would have a child, although they were not necessarily more likely to want a child. Lesbian women stated that it wasn't something they assumed as part of their adulthood because of their sexual orientation, but they did hope while they were growing up that they would be mothers.

Lesbian women identified a number of factors driving their decision to have a child. The most common reason given was that they wanted to have a family and did not believe that a couple alone was a family. One of the women explained,

> Well, I think that every woman wants to have her own family, her own husband or wife and kids. . . . We weren't really a family until the kids came along. . . . I love it all, being a soccer mom, teaching them to walk, helping with homework. . . . It is a kind of love that you don't have with anyone else. I wanted that kind

of unconditional love, someone who would be around when I get old. . . . Plus, having a child too, that cemented our relationship and made us a family. It gave us something to focus on together and share. They are *our* kids. It is something deeply rewarding that we share with no one but one another.

Other women said they wanted to have a child out of a deep love for children. They referred to how much they enjoyed each of their child's life stages. These women identified children as being uniquely innocent and able to bring a joy to the household that adults do not. They referred to their children's infectious laughs and ability to bring their parents great happiness with a simple smile.

Some of the women saw raising a child as a political statement. These women said that having a child was an experience most women had, and they did not want to "lose out" on that experience because of their sexual orientation. They felt they had a right to raise a child just like any other adult and that they should exercise that right. One of the women explained, "People will see that we are just like every other family, every other woman. They will see that we are not deviants, whose kids end up psychotic. . . . Susan and I are there at all of the soccer games, all of the parent-teacher committees. We cannot be ignored . . . or given second best anymore."

When asked if they needed to consider the cost of adoption or fertility treatments in their decisions to have a child, some of the lesbians said the costs were a stumbling block they had to "work through." However, cost did not prevent them from pursuing adoption or in vitro fertilization/artificial insemination when they decided to have a child. A minority of women were given or loaned the money for adoption by their parents. A few had to save for the costs over a year or two to adopt or undergo fertility treatments. A minority of the lesbians and heterosexual women had to argue with their insurance companies to provide fertility treatments, which delayed the beginning of the therapies by several months. None of the couples though allowed cost alone to prevent them from acquiring a child once they decided to become parents.

Heterosexual men and women gave a few additional reasons for having a child beyond those given by the lesbian women. Heterosexuals were more likely to say that having a child was just expected and something that went along with being married. One of the women said, "As soon as we got married, his family and my family started asking when we were going to have kids. Even my friends would ask and say that they wanted to be 'aunts.'" These women felt pressure both internally and externally to have a child and saw it as the next step in their marriages. In contrast, lesbian women noted no outside pressure or expectation to have a child. Nor did they see it as a progression of their marriages, but they did see having a child as necessary for having a family.

Heterosexual men were more likely to want to be a father than gay men. This may have been because of the additional cost of having a child for gay men and the extra work they have to go through to adopt. It may also be due to the fact that heterosexual men have a wife who will be the child's mother, a role that typically includes performing more than half of the work in raising a child. Heterosexual men were more likely to want someone to carry on their name and to say they wanted to experience certain aspects of fatherhood such as teaching the children sports or watching them grow. Gay men did not mention these issues in their decision making.

ADOPTION VERSUS FERTILITY TREATMENTS

Heterosexual couples tend to have their children through conception without technological assistance. Only one of the heterosexual couples had adopted a child. Several other heterosexual couples had relied on in vitro fertilization due to infertility in order to have a child. By and large though, children from heterosexual parents were biologically related to both parents and were conceived through sexual intercourse. Heterosexual couples said they would have considered adopting a child only if they could not have one "of their own."

Gay and lesbian couples need to rely exclusively on nontraditional methods of acquiring a child unless one of the partners has a child from a previous heterosexual marriage. One gay couple planned to adopt a child in the future, but they had not yet considered whether to pursue a domestic adoption or an international adoption. They said their decision would depend on the length of time that the adoption would take, preferring a shorter wait period, and the perceived likelihood of the adoption occurring. They did not wish to pursue any options that might lead to a dead end. Likewise, the couple was not considering surrogacy, which they believed was "risky," and gave too much control to the surrogate mother. The men had not ruled out adopting a toddler, but they preferred an infant and did not want to adopt a child older than three years of age. They also hoped they would not have to adopt a child with physical disabilities, but they believed they could easily cope with a child who had a learning disability. This couple was biracial, and both individuals were open to adopting a child of any race.

Lesbian couples embraced a variety of options that were open to them. The vast majority of the youngest and most educated couples planned not to have children. They said they preferred to focus on their careers, time with one another, and leisure activities in which they were highly involved. Many of the women in these couples were very close to at least some of their nieces and nephews and cultivated those bonds. They said their partners also did not want to have a child. The women were not concerned that they would have regrets in the future and saw this as the best option for them. This preference may be the result of a history in which lesbians could not adopt and a more recent acceptance among society in general of childless or "child-free" marriages.

Other young lesbian couples either were planning to have children with fertility treatments or already had a child vis-à-vis artificial insemination. The wife of one of the women had recently given birth as a result of a brief series of artificial insemination treatments. Kim and Sibyl had decided that Sibyl would carry their first child and stay home with him or her since Sibyl was the one with greater job seniority. Kim intended to carry a second child later for the couple after she was more established in her career. Kim had already legally adopted their child, and Sibyl would do the same later for Kim's child. Kim said it was not essential to the two women that their children have a biological connection to one of them, but it was their preference. Kim stated, "I love that I can look at our baby and see a 'mini-Sibyl.' . . . I think that Sib also feels a connection to her that she would not otherwise. Also, it makes each of us a little more confident that we will know her genetic history if something comes up, or more important, we know that nothing *will* come up." Sibyl and Kim had planned to adopt a child if neither was able to get pregnant. They had not put a limit on the number of fertility treatments that each was willing to forego before giving up, nor how much they were willing to spend for each to get pregnant. They decided to take it one day at a time as they pursued their options, starting with the least expensive choice, artificial insemination. The couple could not identify a male relative or friend that they could ask to be a sperm donor, so they instead chose to use a sperm bank that offered some insurance of a healthy donor with no known genetic defects.

Other young lesbian couples were also intending to pursue fertility treatments over adoption to become parents. They were confident they would get pregnant due to their relative youth. They also explained that this option was preferred to a domestic adoption because biological parents could later change their minds. The women were open to pursuing an international adoption later in time, but they did not have the money to proceed toward that option early on in the process. These couples had been married for less than two years and did not yet have substantial financial resources.

Older lesbian couples are more likely to have adopted children, with the exception of mothers with children from previous heterosexual marriages. Cindy and Sam adopted from within the United States, while all of the other couples adopted internationally. Cindy and Sam originally intended to adopt internationally, but they changed their minds when they became aware of the numbers of children of color who needed homes. Cindy and Sam both wanted an infant, and both preferred daughters. They planned to each adopt one child since second-parent adoption was not possible at that time.[10] Each was eligible for parental leave to adopt, and they were financially secure enough to pursue two adoptions. Although they had originally preferred female infants, they ended up adopting two African American boys due to the higher number of available boys. Sam explained,

> At the time, we were aware of the need to learn about and incorporate African culture into our home . . . and our family culture. We did that from when the boys were babies, and we still do that today. . . . We also knew that we needed to create an extended family around us so that they would have role models like them, other men, other black men that they could relate to. . . . We decided then to move to the suburbs . . . so that the boys could go to good schools, but also schools with other black children so that they did not feel like the token blacks. We looked all around before deciding on the town that we live in now.

The most common route to becoming parents for the lesbian couples was the international adoption of one or more children. Couples adopted children primarily from India, Guatemala, China, and other Asian countries. All of the couples had approached an adoption agency in their area and been forthcoming to the agency about being in a same-sex relationship. The adoption agencies were supportive, and their agents told them not to "look like a couple" at the embassies or when dealing with the directors of the orphanages and foster families from which they were adopting. The reason for this was that the countries all had a law that prevented international adoption from a "knowingly" homosexual person. Each of the countries though practiced a "don't ask, don't tell" policy. One of the mothers stated,

> When we were first together, you would walk the streets of Provincetown and see all of these lesbian couples pushing baby carriages with Chinese babies. Then China cracked down and would not allow single-parent adoptions anymore because they discovered that so many were lesbians. . . . By the time that

we got around to adopting, you could do a single-parent adoption in India. We were honest with our adoption agency. I was terrified that if we weren't, they would find out in the home study anyway, and I, we, did not want to risk anything. . . . They told us that they would present [my wife] as a single parent, and that I lived with her and would provide support. . . . The director had a "don't ask, don't tell" policy. He really did not want to know about it. We were terrified that they would find out though because my legal name was hyphenated. I asked the bank not to use my hyphenated name, but my legal name was on my passport. I thought that the INS would catch it if the director didn't. They only cared about the social security number though.

Sarah and Toni had a similar experience during their second adoption from a foster family in Guatemala. In both instances, the second parent was able to adopt after the child was in Massachusetts.

Sarah pointed out that policies have changed with international adoption. She explained,

First China stopped allowing same-sex couples to adopt. Now India and Guatemala have stopped. People have to lie now to their agencies too. . . . Today lesbian couples are going the route of in vitro fertilization or national adoptions. . . . We did not want to do a domestic adoption because we were afraid that the couple [or biological parents] would change their minds.

THE CHALLENGES OF SAME-SEX PARENTING

Same-sex parents face a number of challenges that heterosexual parents do not. Melissa said that her greatest concern when she left her husband was the effect that her sexual orientation would have on her twelve-year-old daughter. Melissa and her partner did not hide the fact that they loved one another from Melissa's daughter, Lindsey. Melissa shared with Lindsey what she felt her daughter could understand at her age. However, they did not want to make her uncomfortable with her friends, so Melissa had her own bedroom in their house to prevent questions from Lindsey's friends. When Lindsey was in college, she surprised her mothers with a T-shirt that said, "I love my two moms." As they joked about the T-shirt, Lindsey asked her mothers why they had separate bedrooms. Melissa told her daughter that they had done it so that she would not feel uncomfortable. Melissa was reassured that this was no longer necessary though when Lindsey replied, "Get over yourself, Mom. Why would I care who you sleep with?"

Same-sex parents also face homophobia from the parents of their children's friends. Nancy stated that some of her son's friends were not allowed to come to his birthday party. Nancy heard from one of the other parents that at least some of these parents were conservative and had expressed concerns about Nancy and Sue being lesbians. Nancy did allow her son to go to these boys' parties though and hoped the parents would see that her children were just like theirs. Nancy said she and Sue received long stares when they first started attending soccer games with their son but that these stares eventually died down as the other parents became more comfortable with them. Their children's friends, ages eight through ten, had asked why they had two moms. Nancy said the friends seemed to accept her children's explanations that it was because their moms loved one another.

Being from a different race is a challenge for same-sex parents as well. Cindy and Sam went well out of their way to investigate and to include their adopted sons' African heritage into their family culture. Cindy said this was sometimes difficult to do since their own cultures were based on Caucasian figures and symbols. They also believed that their children had been victims of racism in their predominantly white town but that they had moved to that town so their sons would have the best education. The children felt they were sometimes the token blacks in the school, and Cindy and Sam carefully monitored their educations to make sure that teachers were expecting as much of them academically as of their white classmates. Both Cindy and Sam believe that teachers often expect less of black children due to a stereotype that they do not perform at as high a level as white children. They intervened at several times in both of their children's educations and asked their sons' teachers to push them a little harder like the Caucasian students.

Lesbian mothers are conscientious of having a male role model for their sons. Nancy and Sue said they had to rely on Nancy's brother to serve as a role model for their son, which he gladly did. Nancy's brother stopped by their home several times a week to spend time with her children, despite having his own family. Although Nancy was somewhat athletic herself, her brother coached the children in sports. Nancy said her brother will be particularly important for her son as he enters puberty, if her son is uncomfortable talking to her or Sue. However, she tries to maintain open communication with her son.

The greatest challenge for same-sex parents though was dealing with family members who do not support their adoptions or pregnancies. One of the women said her sister-in-law was very vocal in her denouncement of the couple's decision to adopt when she revealed it to the family. Since then she has spent very little time with her sister-in-law and continues to be angry about her reaction. Likewise, Sybil thinks her brother and sister-in-law are racist, so Sybil has been estranged from them for the sake of her African American sons. Only one set of grandparents has no interest in their adopted grandchildren because of their daughter's lesbianism. This set of grandparents has never met their grandchildren and do not recognize them on birthdays or holidays, although they continue to send gifts to their daughter. In comparison, another set of grandparents are so enthusiastic about their daughter's adoptions that they paid for each adoption as a gift.

PARENTING

How then is parenting or raising children for same-sex couples similar to and different from the experiences of heterosexual parents? How do same-sex couples "do parenting"? Same-sex couples were much more likely to share parenting. That is, same-sex couples were more likely to be involved in the same tasks for their children rather than create a division of labor. Both parents went to sporting events and after-school activities. They both gave their babies baths, and both got up in the night to give them a bottle. Both parents cultivated communication with their children and open relationships. In most regards, parental ties were quite similar within each family.

Same-sex couples were also more likely than were heterosexual parents to share decision making over a wide scope of their children's lives. Heterosexual couples usually left decisions about schooling and what the children ate, as well as getting to know their children's friends, to the mother. Heterosexual mothers were also more likely to be responsible solely for getting children to after-school activities, finding resources for learning disabilities, and shopping for clothes and gifts. Same-sex couples, especially lesbians, were much more likely to share jointly in all of these decisions and activities.

Similarly, lesbian moms attempt to make sure their children spend a relatively equivalent amount of time with grandparents, including during holidays, assuming that all else is equal. In situations where grandparents were either estranged from the parents or lived far away, couples and their children spent more time with only one set of grandparents. Nancy had to explain to her children that they did not know their grandmother because she was upset with Nancy and not with them. She said it was a difficult conversation to have with her children because while she wanted them to know that their grandmother's estrangement had nothing to do with them, she also did not want them to feel any shame about their mothers' relationship.

Heterosexual couples were much more likely to have one of the parents stay at home with children. This was particularly true for older couples. Only one of the lesbian couples had a stay-at-home mom. After further discussion though, it became clear that this mother was staying home for medical reasons as well.

Lesbian couples tended to communicate extensively with their children and to provide them with adequate explanations for their decisions. They were thoughtful in their choices for disciplining, preferring to give their younger children "time outs" and withholding privileges for their older children. The mothers tried to give their children options and encouraged them to choose their options wisely. Mothers said they focused on being consistent with their children and aimed to provide them with stability.

Many of the adopted children had learning disabilities. Mothers said it sometimes caused problems with extended family that were not patient with the children. Sue, for example, said she had recently been avoiding seeing her mother with the children because her mother was judgmental about her son's attention deficit hyperactivity disorder. Lesbian mothers were knowledgeable of their children's rights for accommodations at school for their disabilities. Most of the learning disabled children had a tutor that their parents paid for and some form of an individual education plan (or IEP) that included goals specific to their level of ability. In contrast, none of the heterosexual parents mentioned having a child with a learning disability.

Same-sex couples often put their children first when they made major life decisions. Cindy and Sam, for example, moved from their comfortable townhouse in the city to live in the suburbs for the benefit of their children's educations. Many of their friends were also chosen with an eye to creating an extended and diverse family for the boys. Likewise, Kim continued to live in the same town as her ex-wife to effectively coparent their daughter, despite her wish to live closer to her new partner. In contrast, heterosexual parents did not seem quite as likely to put their children foremost in making major life decisions. This may have been because their children did not have as many special needs as the adopted children of homosexual parents. Social structures, such as schools, have been set up to meet the needs of the typical heterosexual nuclear family. While all schools are supposed to provide accommodations to children with special needs, these services are not always readily available. Instead, the expectation is that individual families will meet their own needs.

In sum, same-sex couples, especially gay men, are less likely to have children than heterosexual couples. This is in part because it requires a conscious choice to parent, rather than being the by-product of an "accident" or just assumed, and because of the arduous process of adoption. While parenthood is not expected of same-sex couples, it is assumed for heterosexual couples. Likewise, gay and lesbian lifestyles often include a greater focus on careers and the couple rather than raising children. To this extent, same-sex marriage does indeed challenge what marriage means by normalizing the decision to focus on the couple and their needs as well as challenging *how* one "parents." Same-sex couples "do parenting" together and share the tasks of parenting to a much greater extent than do heterosexual couples, who leave many of the parenting tasks to the mother. As a result, parenting can be a more enjoyable experience for same-sex couples despite the cost of adopting a child or undergoing fertility treatments.

Same-sex couples choose whether to adopt or seek fertility treatments based on what is most likely to provide them with a child in the near future. Couples do not allow the cost to deter them, although younger couples postpone getting a child until they are financially stable. Same-sex couples face several challenges that heterosexual couples do not, the greatest being the denouncement by extended family members of their choice to parent a child.

So far we have looked at the effect of being in a same-sex marriage on relationships with parents and the implications for raising children. The next chapter will consider the effect on the couple and the implications of homosexuality for their marriage. It is intended to give parents insight into the marital experience of their gay or lesbian children.

Chapter 7

The Effect of Sexual Orientation on the Couple's Marriage

Chapter 4 looked at the impact of being gay or lesbian and same-sex marriage on one's relationship with parents. Being homosexual and the homophobia and lack of support that go with it will affect the couple and their marriage too. Statistics show more divorce and dissolution of relationships and lower rates of marriage among same-sex couples than among heterosexuals.[1] Gay couples, unlike heterosexual and lesbian couples, are also less likely to maintain a monogamous relationship following marriage.[2] Gay men do become more monogamous once they marry, although not to the level of monogamy for heterosexuals and lesbians.[3]

It is not surprising that same-sex couples are more prone to marital dissolution and divorce than heterosexual couples. Same-sex couples receive less parental and institutional support than do heterosexual couples.[4] As such, they are under greater stress in marriage. In fact, interracial same-sex couples state that their sexual orientation is more stressful than being mixed race. Same-sex couples also experience the homophobia that continues to exist in America, which may be exacerbated by their marriage and any visible display of their love for one another. Same-sex partners cannot fall back on gendered assumptions of what marriage means.[5] While this allows couples to create their own versions of marriage, it also means that couples will have less guidance and expected patterns to rely on in establishing their relationship. This may add stress and anxiety to the first years of cohabitation and marriage.

However, there are some reasons to be surprised that same-sex marriages have higher rates of divorce and separation and lower rates of marriage. Because the option of marriage has only recently been available in certain states, same-sex couples tend to marry later in life, which typically decreases the likelihood of divorce.[6] Waiting to marry allows the relationship to unfurl and develop over time. Many same-sex couples had commitment ceremonies prior to marriage. While not a legal marriage, a commitment ceremony gives a sense of permanence and security to the couple. Same-sex couples also experience greater sharing in their marriages and are more likely to have egalitarian relationships, which would decrease the likelihood of divorce.[7] While same-sex couples are not expected to marry, it is seen as a logical and expected progression of the relationship for heterosexuals. Because of these and possibly other factors, gay and lesbian couples tend to be quite similar to heterosexual couples on measures of relationship health.[8] Gay and lesbian couples did not differ from heterosexuals on this measure for half (50 percent) of the comparisons. Gay and lesbian couples actually functioned better than heterosexual couples in 78 percent of the couples where there was a difference.

REACTIONS OF FRIENDS AND FAMILY

The reactions of friends and family have a profound effect on the romantic relationships of the gay men and lesbians. Several discussed having to give up earlier relationships because of their parents' initial reactions to their sexual orientation. Maria, for example, had discontinued earlier relationships because her parents were so adamantly opposed to her being with another woman. Maria explained, "I had another girlfriend, another serious girlfriend, before this. My parents, and brother, said that they could not accept it though. I did not want to have to give up my family—to stay together. . . . Eventually it just got to be too much, too much fighting. We broke up. . . . No, it was not a conscious decision. It was just too much, stress all around." Other individuals likewise said it was the stress that overturned earlier relationships, stress that resulted from arguments with their parents about their relationships and sexual orientation. For some individuals, their disclosure to their parents occurred at the same time as these relationships were developing or was the result of these relationships. Some parents had deliberately intervened in the romantic entanglements of young adults, especially those living at home. Steve said, "My stepfather would not allow any of my male friends to come home. There was one person. . . . I wish that it had really worked out with him. He was certainly the best. . . . He treated me the best of everyone I have known or been with." Likewise, Ben stated, "My dad would never have let me have an open relationship if I still lived at home. I would have been afraid to be seen with anyone, to be myself. That is why I moved away. . . . When I was in high school, I couldn't have a boyfriend. He made that perfectly clear."

The reactions of parents also affected the relationship between same-sex partners when one partner did not stand up to their family for the needs of the other partner. For example, Kim was outraged when her wife, from whom she is now divorced, allowed her family to treat Kim as a typical roommate rather than as a spouse. She described her sister-in-law coming to visit and not including Kim when she and Chris, Kim's wife, went shopping for furniture for their new home. Kim said that neither of them even consulted with her and treated her as a tenant in their home. Kim later talked to Chris about this but said "that she never did get it." Kim said this added to the problems that she had with her wife but that it was not the cause of their divorce. Likewise, Ben said he and his husband, Casey, argue over the fact that Ben does not bring Casey home with him when he visits. Ben said his mother would be okay with Casey visiting, although he does not know how she would feel about them sharing a bedroom in her house. Ben's father, however, has not even met Casey. Ben said,

> We argue about it, a lot every time that I am planning a trip. My dad is my dad. He is not going to change. He is not going to accept this, but I want to have a relationship with him. . . . What I tell Casey is that I have chosen him over my dad and living [back] there. I *have* put our relationship first, but I don't want to—totally exclude my dad either.

In contrast, Nancy's wife, Sue, had a very different reaction to her mother-in-law's unwillingness to accept her as Nancy's wife. Nancy tried very hard to encourage her mother, Arlene, to recognize Sue and their children, to ask about them during phone calls, and to include them in holiday greetings. Nancy was equally as distraught about Arlene's reaction to Sue and the children as Sue was, but they did not argue. Perhaps this was because Nancy visited no more often than every seven years and did not call more often than every four months. In other words, she curtailed her relationship with her mother for the sake of her spouse.

The *potential* for family discovering that he was gay prevented one of the men from even introducing his partner to his grown children. Bob was so uncomfortable with his sexual orientation that he did not dare to allow his children to find out about it. His spouse, Darryl, encouraged Bob to disclose his homosexuality both to his children and to his coworkers. Bob though said it was harder for him to do than it was for Darryl because he is older and from a different generation where there is greater homophobia. Bob did not know how his children would react to this disclosure, but he believed they would at least be uncomfortable with him and possibly reject him.

SOCIETAL CONCERNS

The extent of homophobia in American society also affected the same-sex couples. Concerns about the reactions of others kept lesbians and gay men from publicly being a couple. Bob hid his sexual orientation from not only his children but his coworkers as well. Bob and his husband, Darryl, did not live near their place of work or near their families, although Darryl had come out to his parents. Bob and Darryl did though have a circle of gay friends with whom they shared their identity. Bob said he was "scared to death" that people at work would find out, even in 2012. He shared the following:

> I am worried that I am going to be found out. I am worried that I will lose my job. People where I work, they are gay bashers. They are not going to let me work there. . . . Either that, or they will make it so hard that I won't *want* to work there. . . . They will say stuff, give me a hard time. It is hard enough as it is . . . now. They make jokes about gays, call them fags. . . . I laugh because I know that it is expected of me, but I am dying inside.[9]

Homosexual couples were also disconcerted about being unable to express their love in public. Jackie explained,

> So many times, I want to be able to reach across and give Linda a kiss, pat her on the toosh, or hug her. You can't though because you know that people are going to stare. They may even say something, something hurtful, and you don't want to expose yourself like that. . . . It is a lot easier with our family because we know that they won't say something, but we don't want to make them uncomfortable either. . . . Face it, straight people *are* uncomfortable when they see men being intimate with men, or women being intimate with women.

DIVORCE

Only a minority of the men and women divorced during the ten years since marriage became an option. Rachel said it was her wife's inability to sustain a relationship that ended their marriage. Although she could not be certain that their sexual orientation had added to their problems, she did believe that her wife's insecurities resulted, in part, from the challenges of being a lesbian in today's society. Rachel said, "I think that Suz had a hard time with staying in the relationship. She ultimately destroyed it because she was so worried about it ending . . . she was so insecure. Every little thing set her off . . . and then she became bitter. . . . I think it is very hard for her. She is very butch, in a society where that is not the norm. . . . So it comes out in her insecurities."

One of the gay men, Rod, had been married to a bisexual. He said it was his partner's continued questioning about his sexual orientation that led to their divorce. Ultimately, Rod's partner had an affair with a woman and left Rod. He and the woman later married, although he and Rod continue to have a sexual relationship. Rod added, "It is really tough being gay. You are supposed to be a swinger, to live the gay life. There is a lot of pressure. . . . I can imagine that it is even harder to be bi, or to be a drag queen, where there are other expectations as well. . . . It is just so much easier for him to be in a straight relationship. He wants to be with me too, and his wife does not seem to mind."

Finally, Kim and her wife divorced after being together for twenty years, fourteen years after their commitment ceremony and six years after their marriage. Kim did not elaborate on the cause of their divorce, but she did say that her in-laws' unwillingness to treat her as [Chris's] spouse and not just a roommate added to their problems.

MONOGAMY

Earlier researchers have looked to see whether or not gay men become more monogamous following marriage.[10] This is part of an effort to investigate whether or not same-sex marriage changes the meaning of marriage. Interestingly, the gay men in both the married and nonmarried couples were not monogamous, suggesting that the meaning of marriage is different for gay couples than for heterosexuals.[11]

In this study, only a very rare minority of the gay men stated that they or their partner continued to be in multiple sexual relationships following marriage. Many, but not all, had been monogamous prior to marriage as well. In contrast, all of the heterosexual men in the study claimed to be monogamous following marriage, but several had multiple girlfriends simultaneously prior to marriage.

Lack of monogamy can provide multiple challenges to marriage. In particular, marriage may not provide security if there is no monogamy. It will weaken a sense of trust and the permanence that are associated with marriage if one person is not in full agreement with the rules of the marriage.

The lack of monogamy may not be detrimental to the marriage though if both partners are comfortable with having multiple sexual partners. In this instance, the security and trust would need to come from a shared understanding of the elevated importance of their own relationship over that of other sexual partners. If this is the case, same-sex marriage could change the meaning of marriage without changing the advantages of marriage.

MENTAL HEALTH AND THE FEAR OF AIDS

Assessing the mental health of lesbians and gay men is beyond the scope of this study. It should be noted though that one of the gay men felt that his stepfather's lack of tolerance for his homosexuality has resulted in his mental health problems. Steve was receiving disability payments from Social Security due to mental health concerns. He attributed these issues to the nervousness that resulted from his stepfather's treatment of him when he was younger. According to Steve, his stepfather believed he could "butch him up" and end his homosexuality by instilling fear in Steve on the ball field. Steve explained,

> He tormented me. He would take me to the ball field and just drill the balls at me. He would call me a sissy and throw the next one even harder if I missed one. . . . Then he would tell me to run bases and throw the ball at me while I ran, *hard*. I wasn't good at sports, and I wasn't good at this. It was just awful. . . . I would dread it, him doing that. . . . It wasn't all of the time, just when he wanted to bully me.

Dominic's mother, Colleen, also believed her son's mental health had suffered as a result of his homosexuality. Colleen stated that it was the way Dominic's peers treated him that had caused his "personal problems," including being a "drag queen." She explained, "I think that Dominic is out there roaming the streets in all of his regalia as a way of saying to people, 'You cannot hurt me anymore. You cannot bring me down.' However, he is going to get himself killed walking along the streets like that at 2:00 am. It is one of the things that I try to get him to talk to his counselor about."

Finally, one of the mothers described her son's alcoholism and drug abuse as being due to his father's rejection of him and his sexual orientation. Ryan had even married and raised two children as part of his denial of his homosexuality. After years of trying to live a straight life though, he began abusing drugs and alcohol. Ryan's wife divorced him, and he turned to a gay lifestyle. However, he continued to abuse alcohol and drugs, perhaps because his acceptance of his homosexuality came with some degree of guilt and self-loathing. At the time of the study, Ryan had been in a rehabilitation facility for several months.

None of the gay men were concerned about contracting HIV. Steve though said that the only reason he was not concerned was that he practiced safe-sex techniques (i.e., condom use) since his partner (his former spouse) had multiple partners. He later admitted, however, that he sometimes did not use a condom when he and his partner "got carried away." He then added, "Maybe I should be concerned, but I have been okay so far." The middle-aged men all had friends who died from AIDS, although the younger men did not. Ed said, "No, I don't worry about contracting the virus, but I can't believe that I never got it. It is just by the grace of God. I was sexually active at a time when the virus was unknown. We didn't use safe sex. We didn't know that we had to. . . . So how did I not get it when so many others did?"

The parents of married gay men were still concerned that their sons would contract HIV. However, they were not as concerned as they had been before their sons married. Colleen explained,

> I think that my son and his husband are faithful . . . that they are not part of the gay scene. . . . But, how do I know? I mean, really, they are not going to tell me that. So yes, I still worry. . . . It is not like I used to worry though when he was single, or when he and my son-in-law first got together. Then I worried all of the time, even though he said that he always used a condom. I mean, what mother would not worry?

Gary's response was most typical of parental comments though. He said, "Kyle is a responsible man. I was worried, but I know that safe sex has been drilled into him from us and the schools from the get-go. . . . Yeah, I worried *more* when I found out that he is gay, and we talked about how he had to be that much more cautious, and responsible as a result." Likewise, all of the parents of gay men said they talked to their sons about using safe-sex practices with greater urgency after learning they were gay.

INSTITUTIONAL SUPPORT

Members of the same-sex couples were asked to identify those institutions in American society that do and do not support their homosexuality. The most common institution reported as *not* providing support was the Catholic Church. Many of the couples were very disappointed that their priests did not support their relationship, although there was one priest in the area who did uphold homosexuality and same-sex couples. These couples believed they were not allowed to follow their faith while also living their true sexual orientation. Several of the couples either stopped attending a church altogether or turned to the local Unitarian Universalist church, which did support their sexual orientation. The following statement best exemplifies the overall reaction on this subject: "I am Catholic. I would really like to attend a Catholic church and receive the sacrament. I miss my faith. . . . The Unitarian Universalist church—has been like a placeholder, as far as my faith goes. I would rather go there than nowhere, but I would also rather that the church bless my marriage." Members of several of the lesbian couples visited multiple churches in search of a priest who might be supportive, but they were always disappointed to learn that the priest would not put aside the position of the Catholic Church to support them.

Lesbians and gay men also identified a variety of services that support heterosexual marriage only. For example, many of the lesbian women stated that the marriage counselors in the area all specialize in heterosexual couples and are unfamiliar with advising and counseling the particular needs of the homosexual community.

Women also pointed out that the popular culture is geared toward the heterosexual community. Jackie, for example, indicated that it is often difficult to find an anniversary or wedding card for a same-sex couple. Likewise, they said that wedding planners and wedding traditions are also heavily weighted toward heterosexual couples and leave the homosexual community feeling marginalized.

Several of the women also pointed out that the institution of marriage and its accompanying roles do not provide them with guidelines for managing their lives. Sue explained,

> Marriage, at least Christian marriage, provides clear roles for the husband versus wife. But what about when there are two wives? Is one of us supposed to be the wife and one be the husband? That does not work for us though. There are two wives, but how does that translate then into who does what or who is what? . . . It offers no guidelines. . . . We are equal partners, but I don't think that Christian marriage supports that.

Likewise, Rachel added,

Sometimes it feels like we are reinventing the wheel, that is, what it means to be married. . . . All of the couples that I know were friends first. . . . Some have other people who are their *best* friends though, just like heterosexuals. For many though, their spouse is their best friend, and they don't have that confidante elsewhere. . . . They don't have all of the supports that heterosexual women do.

Homosexual couples share more, and their relationships are more egalitarian.[12] Most of the lesbians and gay men in this study agreed with this statement and believed that this quality greatly improved their lives and their marriages. Kris explained,

We do everything together . . . we share everything. That deepens the relationship between us. We are not only lovers, but we have a deeper understanding of the other person. . . . We are from different denominations, but we are equally religious and equally knowledgeable about the Bible, and that makes our relationship so much better. . . . We share all of the jobs around the house, and that makes our home life much more meaningful.

The lack of gendered assumptions of what marriage means and the inability to fall back on traditional roles then has an overall positive effect. However, couples have to invent what marriage means for them or define it for their own relationship, which leaves some believing that the institution has somewhat failed them. The lack of clear gender roles also means less available information on the expected parameters of their relationships with people outside of the marriage, such as other friends and in-laws. This uncertainty adds additional stress—but for only a minority of the same-sex couples.

DIFFICULTIES IN HAVING CHILDREN

Homosexual marriages require that the couple adhere to a long and onerous process in order to have a child. Those couples that adopted children all spoke of the stress that the adoptions put on their marriages. Most individuals, however, believed they had supported one another through the process and had received support from family and close friends. In particular, the costs of the adoptions and the concern that the adoption would not go through put the couples on "pins and needles," sometimes for multiple years. None of the couples that tried to adopt had been unable to do so. Likewise, all of the childless couples had deliberately chosen not to have children rather than foregoing the option due to costs or the requirements of the process. That is, being in a same-sex marriage did not preclude couples from having a child if they wished to do so.

Only a small minority of the lesbian couples underwent in vitro fertilization. Chloe said that although they were anxious for Zena to conceive, it did not have a deleterious effect on their relationship. She explained, "If anything, it brought us together more—because we shared it—the first ultrasound, the birth, the naming. It could have been stressful if we, she, had a harder time conceiving. But the good outweighed the bad by far." Other couples that conceived through this means shared similar experiences. They also added that they would have turned to adoption if fertility treatments had not worked. None of the couples that adopted had undergone fertility treatments earlier, however.

ADDITIONAL EFFECTS ON THE COUPLE

Couples overwhelmingly pointed out that being married finally gave their relationships equal status to those of heterosexuals. It allowed them the opportunity to "just be themselves." They saw this as having an enormously positive impact on their relationship. One of the men said,

> Finally we don't have to hide our relationship. The state has confirmed that it is okay for us to be together, that there is nothing wrong with it. We get to have all of the benefits that come with marriage. . . . It is just a huge thing to be able to be who we are and not have to be ashamed. . . . I think that it has also hugely affected our relationship because it is no longer stigmatized like that.

Individuals used phrases such as feeling "less stressed," "more legitimated," "less worried [about legal and financial rights]," and "more secure" in their relationships in general as a result of being married. They said they were not necessarily more confident that the relationship would be permanent (since they were already confident of that), but they believed it would be easier to maintain the relationship with the supports they had.

Gay men and lesbians believed they benefited from their relationship unfurling prior to marriage. All but a minority of the couples were in their current relationship for a lengthy period prior to marriage, but only because marriage was not an option earlier on in the relationship. Most had a commitment ceremony prior to their marriage as well. The fact that they were older when they married and there was a longer period that they were together made the couples feel their relationships were more solid and that most of the problems in their relationships were addressed prior to marriage. One woman said, "In a lot of ways, our relationship did not change when we got married because we had been together so long. . . . I mean, it did change in that we got the benefits and felt like our rights had been validated. But it is not like we are teenagers just starting out." Couples believed that the extended years prior to marriage meant they had an opportunity to get to know one another more fully and sometimes even over multiple stages of the person's life. They had the chance to grow together and to work out their differences. They had also developed into more mature adults who were capable of problem solving and who had more secure financial resources.

In sum, being in a same-sex marriage has an important effect on the relationship and on the couple. The biggest impact, from the perspective of the men and women, is the negative effect on their relationship and earlier relationships when parents were not supportive or did not treat their partners well. In addition, the homophobia and assumption of heterosexuality that saturate America made it difficult for couples to express their relationships publicly in a way that heterosexual couples could. Heterosexuals have the luxury of sharing the elevated status of their relationship with others while same-sex couples do not. Gay men and lesbians are careful even around family not to make others uncomfortable, which inhibits their relationship with one another and sometimes with family as well. Likewise, the difficulty in having children puts a strain on each member of the couple but does not drive a wedge between them. Instead, couples believe they support one another through the process. Not being able to fall back on gendered assumptions of their marital roles allows couples to have better relationships and to share more of those roles. While this takes extra "work," couples feel that overall it is a positive outcome. As a result, same-sex marriage appears to be changing the nature of marriage in at least some respects. Parents then can expect that their gay and lesbian children will have marriages that are simultaneously improved and challenged by their homosexual orientation.

Chapter 8

Same-Sex Marriage and the Extended Family

The work that has been done on the effects of homosexuality on the family of origin looks at the impact on the relationship with one's parents.[1] However, disclosure of homosexuality, bringing a same-sex partner into the family, and same-sex marriage will also impact relationships with the broader extended family.[2] As such, the impact of same-sex marriage on the extended family must also be considered. Relationships to extended family do matter to one's social world and sense of belonging even though individuals usually do not feel as close to grandparents, siblings, aunts/uncles, and cousins in comparison to parents and one's own children.[3] For example, a sense of belonging and participating in extended family rituals has been shown to be important for black lesbians.[4] This chapter will look at the effect of being in a same-sex marriage on extended family relationships for both gay men and lesbians and thus complete the overall picture of effects on the family. It is intended to help parents better understand the reactions of the wider family to their child's sexual orientation and same-sex marriage.

REACTIONS OF EXTENDED FAMILY

The reactions of extended family to same-sex marriage depend on a number of factors. This includes the type of relationship (whether a grandparent, sibling, aunt/uncle, or cousin) and thus how far from the inner family the relationship extends. Grandparents and siblings were most likely to support the couple and to accept the family member's sexual orientation. Some aunts and uncles were also supportive of gay nieces and nephews, but it was for the benefit of their sibling. Those aunts and uncles who were not supportive were usually highly homophobic, which was the second factor that affected the reactions of extended family. Cousins, the least close of these four relationships, varied in their responses. Their reactions to their cousin's same-sex marriage depended mostly on their earlier history with one another. This will be described in greater detail below.

Grandparents

Grandparents were typically supportive of their grandchild's homosexuality and same-sex marriage. They welcomed same-sex spouses into the family similar to their heterosexual grandchildren-in-law. Only rarely did a grandparent's homophobia prevent them from accepting their grandchild's sexual orientation. Sandy, for example, explained,

> My father's mother, well, she's never really accepted Claire [Sandy's wife]. . . .
> I heard through the family grapevine when we first sent out wedding invitations
> that she was not going to come to the wedding or send a gift, and she didn't.
> That was okay with me. . . . My father's side of the family is just like that. . . .
> There is a lot of hatred on that side. My dad told me that my grandma was negative when he told her that I am gay too, but he did not go into any of the details.

After three years of marriage, Sandy's grandmother still has not acknowledged her marriage to Claire. She sent holiday cards to Sandy only and has never asked to meet Claire. When asked how Sandy and Claire feel about this, Sandy explained, "Well, we figure she is old and from a different generation. I wish that she felt different, but I don't see her that much either. It won't change her if I make a big deal about it. . . . We weren't that close to begin with. . . . I did not see her that much when I was growing up. . . . But she is the only grandparent that I have, so I don't say anything." In contrast, Ben gave the following account:

> My grandparents have been great. My mom's parents, I am closer to them actually, but they were the ones that had to get used to it—to me being gay and
> getting married. At first, they were like, "Oh, no." They were, uncomfortable
> around me, formal like. It was like they did not want to touch me. . . . They just
> had to get used to it though. . . . Now things are not really like they used to be
> exactly, but I think that they are mostly used to it. They talk to him [Ben's husband] when they call, and they send us both gifts. They came to our wedding. . .
> . I think that they came around because they love me. Things had gotten weird.
> . . . My other grandma, my dad's mom, she is much cooler about it than my dad
> is even. She told me that it is okay with her and something that she can accept

as long as I am happy. . . . My sister though told me that she [the grandmother] told her that she wished I would change my mind though, like I could do that.

Several parents said they had to be careful not to jeopardize the grandparent-grandchild relationship when they shared their child's sexual orientation with their own parent. Consider the example of Sally:

I was so worried about telling my mom. I did not want to harm her relationship with my son. They have always been so close, and he loves her so much, and she loves him so much. I did not want him to have to deal with her being upset with him on top of everything else. She was great though. She was clearly surprised, but she said that it was fine and that she would love him no matter what.

Siblings

Most of the men and women in the study believed that their siblings were supportive of their marriages with a few exceptions. Joan was one of those exceptions. She explained,

My brother and his wife, I mostly stay away. I call my brother, very rarely though, to talk to him about our mother. Mostly though, I just stay away. . . . They are very racist and homophobic. I don't want our daughter [who is of a different race] around them. Even before then though, I was offended by how homophobic they are. I know that it comes from my sister-in-law's background and her family's religion, but still.

Karen also believed that one of her three sisters did not support her marriage because of her attitudes toward homosexuality. She said, "When I told her that we were getting married, she just shrieked. She kept yelling, 'How can you? It is a sin. It is not too late to repent. You can't get married.' I know it comes from her religion—that it is being fed to her. But she is my sister. How can I love her when she spews such hate?"

In contrast, the other men and women said that their siblings went well out of their way to be supportive. Jackie said,

I am from a big French Canadian family. All of my siblings have supported us. They make Linda feel very welcome. They go well out of their way to do so. It makes me love them so much more. For example, they check and double-check that she is always included in things for us women in the family. . . . They make sure that they remember her birthday, our anniversary—more than they do for the brothers-in-laws. They do everything that they can to make her feel welcome.

Kris also said that his three younger siblings have been supportive, despite his parents' vehement opposition to his sexual orientation and to his marriage. Although he appreciated this support and the fact that his siblings gave it to him against their parents' wishes, it still did not "make up" for his parents' rejection of him. He explained, "My younger brothers and sister have been great. . . . They will meet us for dinner or just to talk . . . and I *know* that my parents forbid it. I really appreciate that. It means a lot to me. . . . I know that they can't convince my parents to change their minds. . . . I just wish that we had my parents' support too."

Aunts and Uncles

For the most part, gay men and lesbians said that their aunts and uncles supported their decisions to marry. However, this support was as much for the benefit of their siblings as it was for their nieces and nephews. Those uncles who were not supportive were members of the clergy and believed they could not endorse the marriages as such. Men and women were very grateful when aunts and uncles attended their wedding and interpreted it as support for their marriage. One of the uncles, for example, was a priest. He believed he could not endorse his niece's marriage since same-sex marriage is considered a sin in the Catholic religion, but he did agree not to denounce his niece's marriage to his sister. This was after his sister chided him for not supporting her daughter.

Cousins

Men and women believed that their cousins were the least likely to feel obligated to support their homosexuality. Several of the gay men and lesbians found this hurtful since their cousins are their peers. Ben explained,

> My two cousins, they just piss me off. They have never been out to visit us. They didn't come to our wedding, and they don't come to see me when I am home. . . . I think it is because I am gay. My cousin Sam is a big jock, and he is probably worried that he is going to catch it or that I am going to hit on him. . . . Janeen, I don't know why she is like this. . . . I guess she is as much a homophobe. It is like I am scum, now that I am gay.

Likewise, Elizabeth explained,

> One of my cousins sent out a Christmas card with a family letter. In it, she discussed how sinful she thought the recent laws allowing same-sex marriage are.

This was after we had sent out a card and letter announcing our marriage. . . . I just stopped sending cards to her after that. . . . I think that my aunt understood why I stopped writing to her daughter after that because she had read both letters.

A SENSE OF BELONGING

The vast majority of the men and women felt a sense of belonging to their extended family or families, even as gay men or lesbians. This included attending family rituals such as holiday meals; identifying with family through shared religion, name, and history; and feeling supported. The degree to which they felt a sense of belonging depended on their geographic distance from their family and what their relationship with the extended family had been like over time. Likewise, men and women were more likely to feel they were a part of the extended family if their *parents* were supportive of their sexual orientation and they were not estranged from their parents. Thus, to some extent, relationships with parents served as a necessary connecting link to the rest of the extended family.

Men and women whose parents were divorced said they sometimes identified with and felt a greater sense of belonging with one side of the family than the other. Again, it depended on what their prior relationship with those family members was like. Most though maintained some level of belonging with each side unless their own parents had been estranged from their families. In these circumstances, adult children sometimes had little to no contact with that side of their extended family.

Many of the men and women said that being gay or lesbian made them feel somewhat different from the rest of the family. They said they tend to be more political than other family members as a result of their fight for gay rights and political involvement. These men and women participated in gay pride parades, volunteered for pro–gay rights representatives, and petitioned for the prerogative to marry. Thus, while they knew who was running for varying offices and what they stood for, many had extended family members who did not even vote except in major national elections.

Some of the lesbians stated that they did not always "fit in" with their female cousins or other women in the family. They felt they were often less a part of the mainstream feminine culture. One of the women said,

I just wasn't like my sisters and girl cousins. They knew all of the boy bands and rock stars, and I just wasn't interested. They wore dresses, cared about their hair and nail polish, and were much more "girly girl" than I was. I felt like I just didn't fit in. I fit in more with my male cousins who cared about sports. I was the tomboy in the family. . . . Later I noticed that I wasn't as close to my female cousins as they were [to each other]. That was probably why.

Likewise, some of the gay men stated that they were not as traditionally masculine, as defined by the heterosexual culture, as the male members of their extended family. Stuart, for example, said,

I am not a jock like my brother, my dad, uncle and cousins. I am not good at math like they are, and I am not going to be an engineer like they are. . . . My uncle and cousins, they are gruff marine types. I can tell that they laugh behind my back. . . . Sometimes it makes me not want to be a part of the overall family. . . . But they are the ones who are the a-holes, and I just remember that. . . . I want to see my grandparents and be a part of things, so I just remember that.

INTERACTING WITH HETEROSEXUAL FAMILY MEMBERS

Lesbians and gay men believed their heterosexual family members varied in whether they thought of them as "truly married" (similarly to heterosexuals) or not. Being seen as "truly married" includes being viewed as much more than friends or roommates but instead sharing a life together, being a family, and having a lifelong commitment to one another. Under these circumstances, the family views the union as a genuine relationship like other marriages. The majority of men and women said that most of their family treated them and their spouses as a genuine married couple. One of the men said,

Yes, they treat us just like my brother and sister-in-law. They *get* the fact that we really are a married couple. My parents take [my husband's] needs and desires into account when they make family plans, just like you would any family member. They have put in the effort and time to really get to know him and to love him. . . . They get that they have to consider what he wants when giving me advice or helping me. . . . They know that he is here for the long haul, and they seem happy about it.

Other men and women believed their family members saw them as married but not in all areas of life. Kim, for example, said,

I think that my family realizes that we are married. But the fact that I do not have a husband and children results in treating us differently. My siblings all thought that I should care for my parents when they got sick. They assumed that I did not have responsibilities to my mate because I don't have a husband. It was like she wasn't really my spouse. They do include her in family get-togethers and holiday gifts, though . . . I don't think that they realize that our finances are tied together either.

Couples who believed their family members did not treat them as genuinely married said their family treated them more like very good friends. While relatives invited the partner to family get-togethers, they did not include him or her on gifts or holiday cards. Likewise, while they were welcoming, they did not go out of their way to get to know the spouse. In addition, although they assumed the couple would still be together in the future, they did not recognize the extent to which the couple shared their lives.

Several of the men and women said that the hardest thing was figuring out how affectionate they could be with one another around family members. Jackie said,

My family is great . . . they are very supportive. I can put my arm around Linda in front of my family. I can give her a kiss. I wouldn't give her a long, passionate kiss though. I wouldn't pat her toosh around them. . . . We don't slow dance at family weddings. . . . I wish that I could do that. . . . People are also more, well, cautious around us than they are around my sibs and their spouses. Nobody would say anything personal about us, whereas they might joke about their love lives with one another.

Likewise, Aaron explained,

For me, the question is, "How gay can I be around my family? How much of my real self can I share?" I don't always let my family see the real me, like being OCD [i.e., obsessive compulsive disorder] about wrapping gifts or liking Kelly Clarkson [i.e., a singer usually preferred by young women]. I don't let them see me flirt with Josh or cozy up to him. My sister though—she does with her boyfriends.

HANDLING PROBLEMATIC FAMILY MEMBERS

Gay men and women addressed family members that did not accept them with a variety of tactics. The simplest method used was to discontinue their relationships with extended kin who did not support their relationship. Charlotte, for example, stopped sending Christmas cards and letters to her cousin who was homophobic. This was easier in situations where the relationship was more peripheral to the person's life already. Parents often interceded when the difficulty was with their own siblings or parents. Nancy said her mother spoke to her brother [i.e., Nancy's uncle] who was a priest when he declared he could not support Nancy's marriage. This did not occur in situations where the parents were equally uncomfortable with their child's sexual orientation though.

Some of the men and women directly confronted their family members who did not support their marriages. Rachael shared the following:

> I found out that my aunt wasn't coming to the wedding, and so I just called and asked why. She said that she still hoped that I would change my mind about being a lesbian. I explained to her again that it is not a choice that I have. . . . Then I told her about how much I wanted her to be there, how important it was to me to have my family there. I think that she was really moved by that. . . . She put aside her feelings about homosexuality in favor of our family ties—that meant a lot to me. I was glad that I called.

This tactic, however, did not always have a positive outcome. Several of the men and women confronted extended family members only to have the difficulty between them remain unchanged or sometimes even worsen. Steve said, "I called my brother and asked him why he never visited. He got all defensive and said that he did not like Stan. I think that what he really doesn't like though is that I am gay. He just wouldn't admit it. . . . I was pretty mad, and it ended in a fight. We haven't spoken since then. So I would say that I only made things worse, unfortunately."

VISITS

Gay men and lesbians were more likely than heterosexuals to visit their parents infrequently. Barb, for example, visits her mother no more often than every seven years. Likewise, Maria and Kris are not welcome in their parents' homes until they renounce their homosexuality. Ben is not allowed to bring his husband to his father's home, and Bob has not introduced his children to his spouse. Steve does not visit his mother who lives in the area very often because his stepfather bullied him earlier in life.

In contrast, heterosexual children visited their parents, even if they did not get along well, out of a sense of obligation. One son had not visited his parents in nearly ten years because he learned that his parents were aware of sexual abuse in the family but had not spoken out about it. Thus, heterosexuals visited their families unless there were extreme reasons not to do so.

Homosexual children were also more likely to say that visits with their parents or their spouses' parents were sometimes uncomfortable. For example, Elizabeth said she was very uneasy when her in-laws first visited because they did not support their daughter's lesbianism. Elizabeth described her in-laws' first visit to her and Lydia's home as follows:

> It was like skating on ice for two weeks straight. I was so worried about offending them without even knowing it—putting my arm around Lydia when I shouldn't, calling her "Honey," and stuff. We certainly did not have sex while they were here. Neither of us could relax enough. I knew that they did not approve, and so I was being tested, put on display. . . . I knew that Lydia was under so much stress, and I wanted to support her and make sure that they did not hurt her.

Other gay men and lesbians also said that visits were sometimes uncomfortable and that it usually resulted from their in-laws' discomfort with homosexuality or their unwillingness to embrace their child's marriage.

Heterosexual children also said visits were sometimes uncomfortable, but it was due to prior problems in the relationship or personal differences. One of the heterosexual daughters said,

> My visits with my mother are uncomfortable because I know that she disapproves of some things about me. My house is messy; my life is messy and hectic. She likes things to be controlled and in order. . . . I don't like how she is judgmental about me. . . . Plus, my husband and I are going through some problems. She doesn't know about that, but I know that she has never approved of my husband. So seeing her only makes all of that worse.

Thus, both heterosexual and homosexual couples were sometimes uncomfortable visiting family when those family members did not approve of their lives.

The question of where the couple is going to sleep during visits affects homosexual couples but not heterosexual couples. None of the heterosexual couples said there was any doubt that they would sleep in the same bed as their spouse. Some of the gay men and lesbians though said it was unclear. Kris said,

> When we were first started dating, Sam lived at home. When I visited from out-of-town, I stayed with him and his mother. I told Sam beforehand and I told his mom when I got there, that I expected to sleep on the couch. . . . It was out of respect for her. . . . Once we were married though, we lived with her for a short time while we were looking for a house. Then I said that I expected to be able

to sleep with Sam in his room. . . . But both times it was unclear. I felt that I had to take control and address the issue.

Lesbians and gay men were more likely to feel they were under a microscope when visiting with family members. One of the women stated, "When we visit my brother, I know that he and his friends, all homophobic, are watching every move that we make. It is like they are either going to get some sort of erotic high from seeing me put my hand on her leg . . . or they are going to be justified in their homophobia by seeing us do something 'deviant.'"

Heterosexual couples were also more likely than same-sex couples to say that their spouse was welcome during visits with family. Visits were sometimes as uncomfortable for heterosexual spouses as they were for same-sex spouses though. However, it was taken for granted that they would accompany their husband or wife on a family visit, particularly if it was a lengthy visit. In contrast, homosexual men and women said both that they were less likely to visit with their spouse and that their spouse was not expected on visits to their family. Men and women believed this had more to do with the overall lack of concrete expectations of same-sex marriage.

How much time homosexual couples spent with one or the other set of parents was more likely to be unequal than was true for heterosexual couples. This was mostly due to homosexual couples having greater difficulty with at least one set of parents due to their lack of acceptance of the couple. Homosexual couples were also more likely to live far from at least one set of parents than was true of the heterosexual couples. Sometimes that geographic distance was the result of their emotional distance. While heterosexual marriages include an expectation that time with parents will be equal, homosexual marriage does not include such presumptions. It is an open slate with the opportunity for each couple to determine their own behaviors.

ISOLATED COUPLES

None of the same-sex couples were completely isolated from all members of their extended families. In fact, every couple felt accepted by at least their spouses' or their own parents and extended family. Individuals believed they were sometimes isolated from one side of the family though. Kris, for example, said,

My brothers and sister are not supposed to call me or see me. Our parents have forbidden it. I have seen them a few times, but not much. I don't want to get them into trouble. I cannot talk to either one of my parents before it turns into a fight, and I am not welcome home. . . . Yes, I miss seeing them and my home-town. . . . I love Sam's mother, but it is not the same as being able to see your own family. It would be worse if we did not have Sam's mother though and all of his family.

Likewise, Karen said, "I was unhappy during the period when I was not in touch with my parents. I missed them and hearing about everyone from home. They are my link to the rest of the family—and friends of the family. I had [my spouse], but it was still hard to not have my family too."

FAMILY SYSTEMS

A family is a system, and as such, it is more than the sum of its parts. Emergent properties, or characteristics, arise from the whole. For example, a cake has characteristics that emerge from the combining of eggs, flour, and sugar. Family processes then are the outcome of the entire family system. The entire family will respond to change and not just one member. Any problematic behaviors are entrenched in the family's relational system rather than being due to any one individual. In addition, families have boundaries, although they may be permeable and there may be boundary ambiguity.[5]

This idea of the family as a system can be applied to adult children "coming out" about their homosexuality and the response of parents to their child's homosexual identity and subsequent same-sex marriage. One person's disclosure of his or her homosexuality affects relationships within the family to varying degrees, but not in isolation. The examples above show that the entire extended family is affected, including grandparents, siblings, aunts and uncles, in-laws, and cousins. However, the relationship between parents and children are affected to a greater degree because of their closer ties and the fact that parents see children as reflective of themselves. In addition, the response of parents has a profound effect on how other family members, especially the other children in the family, respond. Kris's parents refused to accept his homosexuality and have pressured their other children to do the same, limiting their time and relationship with Kris. In contrast, Cali's parents have been very accepting of her lesbianism and marriage and likewise so have her siblings.

Problems are entrenched in the way that the family relates to one another. All that it takes is one person's homophobia for the overall family to reject the same-sex marriage. This does not always occur though, as is evidenced by extended family members sometimes being more accepting of the marriage than are parents. Family boundaries are clearly permeable, as is indicated by the fact that children-in-law move into the family system, and children join the system of their in-laws. Some families though do not fully integrate children-in-law into the family or object to their child's movement into their in-laws' family system.

It is the nature of a family that its members are intensely connected emotionally.[6] Family members are so interconnected that it is as if they are living under the same emotional skin. People seek one another's attention, approval, and support. Likewise, they react to one another's needs and stresses so that a change in one person's functioning affects the functioning of others. Any messages or rules that characterize the overall family shape individual family members' behavior toward compliance.

A family's intense connections are exemplified by the extent to which parents respond to their adult child's disclosure of their sexual orientation and the extent to which adult children are affected by their parents' rejection, if it occurs. The above examples also show how family members seek one another's approval and support. A family's message of homophobia may also make some gay men and lesbians try to comply with the expectation of heterosexuality and deny their true orientation, as was the case with Barb's son, Ryan, who tried to live as a heterosexual for many years.

The overall family culture affects its adjustment to a child's or other family member's homosexuality. For example, a family culture of "secret keeping" (also referred to as a "strategy of silence"[7]) prevents the adjustment of all to an individual's disclosure. Likewise, the "family closet" or denial of homosexuality inhibits the broader extended family and family friends from the opportunity to provide support to parents and the couple and to adapt. In contrast, a culture of support and acceptance can permeate the system and encourage the support and acceptance of all members of the system. Clearly, there are pressures on homosexual couples to conform to heterosexual models of family, such as owning a home, whether internal or external. However, it should be pointed out that the pressures to marry and to raise children are not nearly as strong as they are in the heterosexual community, as is exemplified in this study.

In sum, this chapter depicts a broader picture of family relationships for the gay and lesbian community extending beyond parent-and-child bonds across the life course. Relationships with extended family members are affected by same-sex marriage and dependent upon how far out the relationship is from the inner family circle and how homophobic the family member is. Being gay or lesbian makes individuals feel they are different from the rest of the family and may affect visits to family and which set of parents the couple sees more often. Couples may feel somewhat self-conscious with family, even if family members accept their homosexuality. Whether or not heterosexuals think of the gay/lesbian couples as married varies, with many assuming that lesbians have fewer competing obligations from their spouse in comparison to heterosexual women. The next chapter will examine how gay men and lesbians go about performing the tasks involved in their family roles, referred to as "doing family," and discuss the advice that the parents and adult children gave to other families that may be struggling with or first encountering these issues. This is intended to aid parents as they navigate the waters of having a child in a same-sex marriage.

Chapter 9

"Doing Family" and Advice to Families

This chapter examines how people with a different sexual orientation "do family." This term includes how married gay men and lesbians perform their family roles, create a sense of family with others, and maintain family relationships and the family system. In this chapter, I will argue that sexual orientation affects each of these processes. Because of the newness of same-sex marriage, how the couple will perform family roles, such as that of an in-law, and how they fulfill the accompanying functions have not been determined. What family will mean for same-sex couples is also in flux. Whether homosexual couples will necessarily include children and in-laws, similar to heterosexual couples, is still up to individual families. How a same-sex couple then creates a sense of family for themselves is not clear. Likewise, how a same-sex couple will sustain family relationships and the family system, such as how they will maintain relationships to their parents similar to or different from heterosexual couples, is also up to individual families. The chapter will conclude with a discussion of whether same-sex couples "do family" similar to heterosexuals and how they do and do not differ. This will aid parents in better understanding the contours of their child's same-sex marriage.

POWER AND THE DIVISION OF LABOR

Same-sex couples were more likely to share home labor, including childcare, housework, cooking, home maintenance, and laundry, than the heterosexual couples in this study. With a few exceptions, most same-sex couples did not specialize in any particular role, such as that of the homemaker versus breadwinner. Instead, they shared work out of a desire to spend time together and because they saw themselves as being able to equally contribute to each task. That is, they saw themselves as more similar to one another in their ability to perform different tasks than the heterosexual couples did. They see this equal division of labor and sharing of work as only fair, more so than heterosexual couples that espouse the specialization of tasks. Likewise, same-sex couples were more likely to share power and to contribute equally to decision making. Some men and women recognized when their partner knew more about some topic or area than they did. In those instances, they would rely more on that person's information and leave it up to him or her to make a decision. Otherwise though, gay and lesbian couples made decisions in collaboration. For example, Rachael made more of the financial decisions in her family because of her background in business administration. However, she and her wife shared decision making equally in every other area of life. Consider some of the examples of differences between homosexual and heterosexual couples. Rod, a gay man, described the sharing of power and division of labor with his husband as follows:

> Steve and I share everything equally with few exceptions. He likes to garden, so he does more of that than I do, but even that I help with. . . . Anything that needs to get done, we just both pitch in—like cooking and cleaning. . . . It is all about doing things together and wanting to spend the time that we are not working together. . . . Why would we want to be doing different things when we are both home? . . . As for decision making, we make decisions together, both equal. We put the needs of ourselves as a couple first before each individual's wishes and desires. Plus, if there is something that one of us feels strongly about or it is more important to them, then that person's opinion is taken into account more.

Compare this to heterosexual Clyde's description:

> Well, I would say that I make more of the decisions than my wife about the important things, and she makes more of the decisions about the day-to-day things. I mean, I don't need to know everything about what my kids are doing, but I do the husband/father things. My wife can't do everything, so I take my son to soccer practices, and my wife takes our daughter to field hockey. I fix everything around the house and take care of the yard—mowing the lawn, raking, and shoveling. I help the kids with school projects, the dad things.

How though do same-sex couples decide what they want for a family life? Rod pointed out that he and Steve are not trying to "live the life of a heterosexual couple." He explained, "We don't feel the need to do everything like heterosexuals. We chose not to have kids. We do go to church though. We have a single-family house with a yard—it is in the city though, not the sub-urbs. We have family time with our own families and time for one another. We don't have to make time for kids' music lessons and practices though or pay for braces and college." Rod further added that the activities he and Steve focus on are centered around their home, their extended families, and their joint hobbies. He also pointed out that they outsourced certain tasks that nei-ther of them enjoyed doing or had time for, such as the laundry, vacuuming, and shopping, which they do online. Thus, "doing family" for homosexuals may involve more choice than is the case for heterosexuals.

Vicki also said that she and Nancy seek some of the same family activities as heterosexuals but not necessarily all of them. For example, she and Nancy are actively involved in all of the interests that their son and daughter are pursuing. In that sense, they are like heterosexuals. However, they own not a detached single-family home with a yard (like many heterosexuals) but a condominium that has only shared common space outdoors. Vicki said, "We just decided not to spend our time fixing things around the house, or taking care of a yard, or having to save for a new roof. . . . We decided that we do not have to do all that other families do."

PARENTHOOD

As discussed in chapter 6, same-sex couples can only "do parenthood" if they make a conscious decision to have a child, through either fertility treatments or adoption. That is, they have to go through a long and arduous process in order to acquire a child. Parenthood for same-sex couples then is "done" volun-tarily and with extensive planning. Heterosexual couples may find themselves becoming parents involuntarily though, and thus at younger ages. They may not be as financially secure or emotionally prepared for raising a child.

"Doing parenthood," however, requires same-sex couples to acquire miss-ing role models for their children. For example, some of the men and women adopted children from other races. One of the lesbians discussed how she and her wife made a point of including role models from that race in their circle of friends and that they had adopted cultural practices from their sons' race as well. Other lesbian couples pointed out that they brought in role models for their sons, especially with regard to learning sports.

Same-sex couples disciplined their children differently from heterosexual couples. In particular, they were more likely to use the withdrawal of privi-leges or the offering of positive rewards to change behavior rather than using a variety of methods as do heterosexual parents, which included spank-ing. They were also more likely to focus on discussion with children and to explain why their children should do certain things, while heterosexual couples were more likely to use directives and imperatives and were less likely to see a need for extended discussions. These findings, however, may be partly due to higher educational and income levels in the homosexual community.

Homosexual couples were more likely than were heterosexuals to assume their children would go to college and to plan for their children to receive some kind of education beyond high school. This included helping children to receive the extra preparation that they needed in order to get into a post-secondary school and to save for the cost of such. Gay and lesbian parents were also more likely to discuss their expectations for higher education with their children and to monitor their academic progress. White parents of adopted black children were more likely to ask teachers to challenge their children and not to fall back on assumptions that black children perform at lower levels.

"Doing parenting" for gay and lesbian parents also meant they had to teach their children about how their family was different and to alert them to homophobia. One of the mothers explained,

> My son came home crying one day because his friend said we were all going to hell. I had to take him aside and explain to him that his friend was just repeating things that he probably heard his parents say. I told him that some people think that way about families that have two mommies or two daddies, but that they are wrong. I told him that those people just do not understand how much his mommy and I love each other. . . . I had to explain that there is nothing that he has to worry about and that he should tell his friend that there is nothing wrong with having two mommies or two daddies.

INTERGENERATIONAL RELATIONSHIPS

Being part of a gay or lesbian couple also affected how adult children related to their parents or their in-laws. As was discussed earlier, an adult child's marriage can actually improve relationships with parents, more so for same-sex couples than for heterosexual couples. Gay sons feel greater freedom to visit with parents relative to heterosexual sons. This is because gay men, who are less likely to share a gendered division of labor, are also less likely to depend on one another on a day-to-day basis. Lesbian women visited and cared for their parents more than heterosexual daughters did. Their families assumed they were free to do so because there was no husband at home who was dependent upon them. The assumption that same-sex couples do not specialize in a division of labor may have accounted for these differences. It may also be due to extended family seeing same-sex couples as "not really married" the way that heterosexuals are and instead being more like friends or roommates.

Interestingly, there was more tension between heterosexual married sons and their parents than gay men and their parents. Heterosexual men (and their mothers, to a lesser extent) were more likely to say that men had to "step back" from their relationships with their parents following marriage. The assumption was that heterosexual men have to focus on their role as provider for their family following marriage. While many of their wives also worked, wives felt greater obligation to their parents than did men. In particular, they were expected to maintain close ties with their parents following marriage. Wives were also the ones who set the social calendar for heterosexual couples. As a result, the couple tended to spend more time with her family than with his family. The husband's parents experienced this as their sons stepping back from them in favor of their in-laws. As such, there was often tension between sons and their parents following marriage as well as tension between daughters-in-law and their in-laws. At times, this latter tension grew so great that it created even greater estrangement between the husband and his parents.

Homosexuality also affected in-law relationships. The parents of lesbian daughters tended to have closer relationships with their daughters-in-law relative to their sons-in-law from heterosexual marriages. This was due in part to the greater effort that lesbian daughters-in-law put into developing close ties with their in-laws and to the parents' expectation that daughters are closer than sons. Homosexual marriage is allowing adult children to define their roles with parents anew, although the power of gender role expectations continues to prevail in intergenerational relationships.

EXTENDED FAMILY AND FAMILY SYSTEMS

Members of same-sex couples stayed close to their extended family with few exceptions. These exceptions were more likely to occur the further the relationship was from the inner nuclear family and the greater the degree of homophobia existed on the part of the family member. Parents sometimes intervened on behalf of their children if a member of the extended family was not supportive of their child's marriage. Most extended family though chose to support the adult child and his or her parents.

How do same-sex couples relate to their extended family or "do extended family?" Although men and women usually brought their spouse into their relationships with extended family, some chose not to out of fear of what their family would think of them. Bob, for example, has never introduced his husband to his children because he does not want them to know he is gay. Thus, "doing family" with extended kin involved leading a double life for Bob. He pretended to live alone and maintained a rigid barrier between those two lives. Bob's children had the number for his cell phone, which only he answered, but not the number for his home phone, which his partner also answered. They also had never been invited to his home. He maintained that it was much easier for them if he visited them in their homes.

Other lesbian and gay men related to their extended kin similarly to the heterosexual couples. They visited extended family occasionally, especially when it could be included with visits to their parents. They kept in touch vis-à-vis social media, holiday letters, and phone calls. Like heterosexual couples, they tended to be closer to family members of the same gender. For example, lesbians were closer to their female cousins and sisters than to their male cousins and brothers.

Unlike heterosexuals, gay men and lesbians said they had to minimize and sometimes hide their differences from extended family during visits and in communication. For example, Melissa said, "I know that it makes my family uncomfortable to see us hold hands or kiss. So we don't do anything like that in front of them, even though they can do it in front of us. . . . I don't call [my wife] sweetie or put my hand on her arm, things heterosexual couples can do without giving it a thought." Likewise, Ben said, "I try not to be too gay in front of the family . . . my uncles, grandfather, brother. . . . I don't tell them about . . . the fact that I wrap gifts and buy cards. I don't tell them about the great fedora that I found or the retro salt and pepper shakers that I got for the kitchen table. I try not to be too different from them." Thus, "doing family" with extended kin for same-sex couples requires trying to fit within heterosexual standards and minimizing any differences. It was the goal of many progressives that instead of replicating heterosexual patterns, same-sex couples would create new homosexual marriages as an equal and known alternative to heterosexual ones. To some extent they have done this by developing an equal and shared division of labor, and so forth, but they have replicated the heterosexual marriage, in part, as well.

RELATIONSHIPS WITH SPOUSES

Same-sex couples receive much less support in their marriages than do heterosexual couples. This is particularly the case when the person is coming out of the closet to their family while simultaneously introducing their new boyfriend or girlfriend. Gay men and lesbians sometimes argued that the lack of support had at times caused problems in their relationships with their spouses. In fact, one of the women said her wife's inability to stick up for her with the wife's family was one of the factors that led to their divorce, although it was not the only factor. However, having been in relationships with other lovers who did not put the relationship first made the couples appreciate one another more.

"Doing marriage" meant sharing roles, responsibilities, and decision making equally. Homosexual couples approached marriage with an egalitarian mindset and principles. For these couples, neither spouse was exempt from particular tasks although they were more likely to specialize when one person had a particular skill set, such as having a business degree. "Doing marriage" then was all about sharing one's life and being together in as many aspects of one's home life as possible. Spouses were also the main supporters of one another in the process of adoption, which could be very stressful.

Same-sex couples experienced greater freedom in "doing marriage." For example, homosexual men and women were more likely to visit their parents without their spouses and to set assumptions for their marriages irrespective of the expectations of heterosexual couples. That is, they had the opportunity to start with a clean slate and to set the expectations of their marriage anew. Although they were not always guided by the assumptions of heterosexual marriage, homosexual marriages more often did fall within the parameters of appropriate gender norms. For example, parents often felt closer to their lesbian daughters-in-law than to their heterosexual sons-in-law due to the prevailing norm of greater closeness to female relatives than to male relatives.

THE FUTURE OF CAREGIVING FOR PARENTS

One of the questions asked at the beginning of this book is how the relationship between parents and their lesbian or gay adult children might affect the likelihood of caregiving later in life. In 2009, it was projected that there were approximately 581,300 same-sex couples in the United States, a likely underestimate, and that the growth in same-sex couples was outpacing population growth.[1] Thus, a significant number of elders could be affected if estrangement from their adult child, or even ambivalence in the relationship, prevents caregiving later in life.[2]

Results show, however, that individuals in same-sex marriages do not necessarily have worse relationships with their parents and in-laws than do heterosexuals. It is true that "coming out" or disclosure of one's sexual orientation initially creates difficulty with parents. Most parents and adult children, however, are able to work this out, and their relationship improves over time even if it is not quite what it once was. However, gay men often have even better relationships with their parents after marriage relative to heterosexual men. Likewise, lesbians tend to have closer relationships with their in-laws relative to heterosexual sons-in-law. In this regard, it is unlikely that same-sex marriage will decrease the prospect of caregiving later in life and may even improve the likelihood. In fact, three of the older women had provided care for parents at varying levels of assistance. Younger lesbians and gay men were as likely as the heterosexual men and women to say they would consider caring for a parent if they needed assistance. Finally, while there were slightly more homosexual children who were estranged from parents than heterosexuals, it was not an excessively large difference.

ADVICE TO OTHER FAMILIES

Parents and adult children were asked to provide advice to other families, that is, other parents and adult children, in the beginning stages of this process of adjustment and change to the child's sexual orientation. Below I include the advice that parents offered to other parents as well as the advice that married gay and lesbian adult children offered to their counterparts.

Parents Offer Advice to Other Parents

The parents of lesbian and gay children were asked to provide advice to other parents who were newly made aware of their children's homosexuality or whose children were planning to marry (or were newly married to) someone of the same gender. Alan and his wife, Helen, said the best advice they could offer was to attend support groups such as PFLAG. Alan and Helen were devastated when their daughter announced she was a lesbian. Alan said he does not know what they would have done if it had not been for PFLAG. He explained,

It is a sucker punch to the gut, when you find out. All of your dreams for your little girl go up in smoke. . . . You think that it happened only to you and your family. . . . You think it is your fault, something that you did to cause this. Maybe you think that there is something that is wrong with your child. . . . Talking to the other PFLAG parents helps you to get beyond all of that. . . . You discover that you are not alone. There are other parents who are good, honest, hardworking people whose children are lesbian too. It takes away some of the blame. You can share your worries, your prejudices, with people who understand. That is why we became the facilitators [of PFLAG] ourselves for a year and why we are so involved even today.

Other parents and adult children also said that PFLAG had been an important resource for them or their parents. One son said he gave his parents a pamphlet about homosexuality and suggested they attend the PFLAG meetings to dispel any myths they had about homosexuality. Sue said she sent her mother to PFLAG to see that homosexuals are average people "just like everyone else."[3] Sue wanted her parents to have a broader base of gay men and lesbians and their parents from which they could generalize and to which they could relate. Colleen, the mother of a gay son, said the PFLAG meetings helped her to prepare for upcoming issues with her son as he grew up, dated, and married. Thus, many parents gain benefits from meeting with other parents over the long run.

Parents also told other parents that they should support their child when he or she disclosed their homosexuality, when they married, and if they had children. One mother said, "They are still your child, the same person that you have always loved. They need you to continue to love them, especially now." Another parent pointed out, "You need to separate your feelings about homosexuality from your relationship with your child. . . . Don't think about what your child is doing or not doing. Don't let your own feelings about homosexuality affect your relationship with your child. More than being gay or lesbian, they are your child." Another mother said,

The best thing that you can do is to listen, be a good listener. Don't jump in with your opinions or your needs. Remember that you are still the parent, and they need you. . . . They need your support. Maintain eye contact. Nod in agreement. Hug them when they cry. Let your child know that you still love them. You can support your child that way, even if you disagree with what they are doing.

Other parents suggested that it was important to tell family and family friends and to garner support for your child's sexual orientation. One father said, "Your kids are not the only ones who need support. You need support too to make it through. You can't depend just on your spouse either because she is going through the same thing. You need to reach out to others. Most people will be there for you. You will be surprised." Parents point out though that the family may have to deal with homophobia from others. Alan said,

> We have one member of the family that I had to confront because I did not want him saying anything harmful to my daughter. I told him when it became common knowledge among the family that I expected him to support her or to stay away. He was taken aback, but he got the message. . . . I just knew that he would say something because he is so uptight about things like that. . . . I had heard him say other things—things *I* would not say to someone's parent. . . . Then I reminded him again when she was dating and when she was getting married. I just wanted him to know that the rules still applied.

Adult children also offered advice to parents. One of the daughters gave the following advice about a child's wedding: "Be glad for your son or daughter when they get married. Treat it like any other child's marriage. Do whatever you did for your other children. Invite family, family friends, and colleagues. Celebrate your child's good fortune to have found someone that they love. Trust me. It is important to your child that you be joyous and not depressed by their marriage." Another child offered the following insight, also about the wedding:

> Your child is going to be devastated if you don't go to the wedding. They may never forgive you if you don't go, or if you are negative about it. If you can't be happy for them, they may not even invite you, and then you are both going to regret it. Do yourself and your child a favor by going *and* being happy for them. Get them a gift. Welcome your new son-in-law or daughter-in-law into the family too.

Parents also stated that they were happy they had gone to their child's wedding, and they recommended that other parents do the same thing even if it meant setting aside their own feelings about the marriage.

Adult Children Provide Advice to Other Gay Men and Lesbians

Adult children offered advice to others facing challenges in their relationships with family. Jackie pointed out that you need to be patient and realize that your family's acceptance of your homosexuality is a process. Jackie said,

> You have to remember that it isn't going to happen overnight. It is going to take your parents a while to accept the fact that you are gay, then that you are dating, and then that you are getting married. It goes on and on, and it won't

happen instantaneously. . . . So you have to be patient. Give them time. . . . Don't worry that just because they are not happy about it right away that they won't come around. Give them the distance that they need while they work it out for themselves.

Jackie also pointed out that it will help your parents and extended family if you can provide them with resources, such as books on homosexuality or similar pamphlets. She suggested that if possible, to enlist the help of other family members who might be more supportive but to recognize your parents' need for privacy while they come to accept the news. She explained,

> If there is someone else in the family who can talk to them, I would suggest enlisting their help. Like, if you have an aunt or uncle who you think could talk to them for you. . . . Or if one of your brothers or sisters could talk to them for you. . . . Remember though that they are not going to want to let everyone know. Don't go too far outside of their circle of trusted other[s]. . . . You don't want to embarrass them in front of others.

Likewise, Susan added,

> Keep in mind that they are from another generation. Our generation has no trouble. . . . We get that homosexuality is not a choice but that it is a totally acceptable way to be. For them, though, it was something that only "bad" people did. You were a freak and shunned from society. You lost your job. You lost your family. People pointed at you in disgust. . . . Of course they do not want that for their kids.

Kim, who had several girlfriends before marrying, pointed out that you have to introduce your significant other to your parents and extended family very slowly. Kim also disclosed her sexual orientation to her mother well before introducing her first girlfriend to her mother. She explained,

> Recognize that it may take your parents and family a little longer to like your girlfriend, to see that the love is just the same, that the relationship is just the same [as a heterosexual one]. . . . So, take it slowly. Don't expect them to love her right away. . . . Go out to something that does not take too long to begin with, lunch or something. Wait awhile and then do something like that again. And then build from there. Don't start out with a weekend together though. . . . Build on success without biting off more than you can chew.

One of the men pointed out that you have to support your partner. Phil said,

> At first it was really hard for Ed . . . when my father had not yet accepted him. He was upset with me for not defending him more with my dad. He thought that

I wasn't standing up to my dad . . . that it meant that I did not love him. . . . If I had to do it all over again, I would have tried to reassure him all along that the fact that I wasn't shoving my dad's face into it [his homosexuality] had nothing to do with how I felt about him [Ed]. I know my dad, and it would not have helped if I had pushed him and insisted that he invite Ed over, if I had insisted that he accept Ed. It just would have caused a fight and made things worse. . . . I should have explained this to Ed all along though. I did not mean for him to get hurt.

Becky offered the practical advice of seeking therapy while undergoing these transitions. She explained,

I thought that it was really helpful to get professional help when I went through all of this. I mean, you feel like you are *losing* your parents, that they are not going to love you anymore. Then you start to worry that maybe you will lose your whole family. . . . You know that you have disappointed them. It is heavy shit. . . . I think that you should get professional help both when you come out and when you bring "the one" home.

Becky further added that many parents might benefit from accessing professional help as well.

Maria was very clear that adult children have to do what is right for them when it comes to accepting their sexual orientation and marrying someone of the same gender. Maria stated, "Listen to your heart. Do what you gotta do. . . . You will know when it is time to come out of the closet. . . . You will know if you have to put your relationship before your parents. Do it. Don't be afraid. You will be glad."

In sum, people with a different sexual orientation "do family" in ways similar to, but also different from, heterosexuals. Like heterosexuals, many choose to marry during a time period in which there are multiple alternative living arrangements for adults. However, "doing marriage" consists of a greater sharing of responsibilities out of a desire to be together, relative to heterosexuals. Others within the family often see their married lesbian siblings as "free" to fulfill family obligations, such as caregiving, if they do not have a husband at home. Gay and lesbian members of the family have greater freedom to visit parents since there is no prescribed script for marriage as we see for heterosexuals. "Doing parenting" often involves bringing in role models of the opposite gender and perhaps of the same race as their child. Same-sex parents focus on more nonauthoritarian methods of disciplining and raising children. They remain close to extended family. However, they minimize differences between themselves and their heterosexual family members to make their family members comfortable with them. It is likely that the future of caregiving remains safe for most homosexual adult children and their parents, although a minority of parents may risk loss of care if their relationships with their children remain estranged. Thus, homosexual families function similar to heterosexual families but with some differences.

Parents of same-sex married individuals offer advice to other parents. In particular, they argue for supporting children even if you do not like their sexual orientation. They point out that you need to separate your feelings about homosexuality from your relationship with your child and that they are still your child "no matter what." Gay and lesbian adult children told other homosexuals to be patient with their parents and extended family as they adjusted to their newly disclosed sexual orientation and to realize that their parents' acceptance is a process that will unfold over time. They argued that you introduce new partners to parents slowly and that you support your partner if your parents are slow to accept him or her.

Chapter 10

Conclusion

This chapter will summarize for parents how having a gay or lesbian child marry changes their relationship with that child and also sums up all of the varied contours of same-sex marriage their adult child may experience. The book itself is intended as a guide for parents (and others) to understand better the implications of their gay or lesbian child's sexual orientation and the key points in their homosexual child's social life. This chapter will highlight the most important components of that discussion.

Findings are based on my original research and supported by the existing literature. The results come from firsthand accounts of both adult married children and the parents of such to provide a complete view of parent–adult child relationships. This includes two data subsets. The first data set was collected in central Massachusetts around 2009 and was based on twenty-five adult children who had been in a heterosexual marriage for at least two years and twenty-five mothers who had at least one married son and one married daughter in heterosexual marriages. This data set served as the control or comparison group. The second data set was the focus of this book. It was based on forty interviews with fifteen married lesbians, fifteen married gay men, and ten parents of a married lesbian or gay man. These interviews were also conducted in central Massachusetts between May 2012 and December 2013. I conducted and transcribed all of the interviews to ensure consistency.

What do parents need to know about the way that the parent-child relationship changes following significant turning points in the child's lifespan? For a gay or lesbian child, those key points include the child's disclosure of their sexual orientation, the beginning of dating, marriage, and the process of acquiring children. This chapter will address whether same-sex couples reproduce the same relationships and structures as do heterosexual couples or whether they create different forms of family and relationships. For example, do same-sex couples adopt the nuclear family format and have children, or does their family consist of the couple alone? Further, are these new family formations and relationship seen as equal and publicly known alternatives to those of heterosexuals? Same-sex marriages may well result in different intergenerational relationships and in-law relationships that do not follow the script expected in heterosexual marriages. This begs the question of whether or not same-sex marriage reproduces the strain between mother/son and mother-in-law/daughter-in-law relationships as found in heterosexual marriages or whether gay or lesbian marriages can rise above the negative outcomes of traditional heterosexual marriage.

It is expected that being gay or lesbian changes the nature of relationships with parents and the extended family. It does this by changing the gender composition of marriage partners and thus the gender combinations in adult child/parent and child-in-law/parent-in-law relationships. It is predicted that the nontraditional relationships of gay men and lesbians will lead to improved relationships with parents and with in-laws following marriage. As such, it will be argued that in-law conflict often arises from the gendered nature of family relationships. When the mother-in-law (or daughter-in-law) is no longer seen as a competitor for the husband's (or son's) attention and time though, in-law conflict will be avoided. In-laws can be close to their daughter's wife because of the presumed closeness of daughters (and thus daughters-in-law) over sons. Likewise, there will be less conflict with a son's husband because of the presumed independence of men in the family. Gay men are also expected to experience less distance from their own parents than are heterosexual men following marriage due to the lack of a traditional division of labor in gay marriages. Overall, it is expected that the nontraditional relationships of gay men and lesbians will lead to improved relationships with parents and with in-laws following marriage.

The contours of same-sex marriage are also expected to be quite different from those of heterosexual marriage. In particular, it is expected that same-sex couples will "do family" quite differently from heterosexual couples, such as focusing on different family functions, performing those functions differently, or fulfilling roles differently. For example, it is anticipated that having spouses of the same gender will change the division of labor in the home and the sharing of power, but how? It may even create greater gender equality and lessen the extent to which marriage is a "greedy" institution that limits relationships with extended family and the broader community. In addition, this chapter will look at how same-sex couples "do parenting" and how that differs from heterosexual parents. Under what circumstances do same-sex couples have children, discipline and raise them, and compensate (if at all) when there is an absence of a parent who is of the same gender or race as the child?

This final chapter will also discuss the particular challenges that same-sex couples face. The other differences that may arise from same-sex marriage include differences in the timing of marriage and the dissolution of relationships. Likewise, the chapter will address differences in the type and extent of support that same-sex couples receive, including both familial and institutional support.

THE NATURE OF PARENT–ADULT CHILD RELATIONSHIPS

Heterosexual daughters tend to remain close to parents throughout adulthood. This may in part be due to the societal expectation that female relatives will remain close to their birth families, especially parents. Daughters also stay close to parents because they set the couple's social calendar and tend to feel more comfortable around their own families. As such, they make more plans with their own parents than with their in-laws. Heterosexual sons, however, tend to be more detached from their parents, according to both the sons and the mothers. Sons say they have to "step back" from their natal families in order to focus on the provider role for their own families. Their roles as husband/father are also less compatible with their role as son relative to the compatibility of women's roles as wife/mother and daughter. That is, women simultaneously fulfill their roles as mother, wife, and daughter by being a conduit for relationships between their children, spouse, and parents. Sons are particularly detached from their families if their parents do not get along well with their wives. Daughters tend to remain close to parents though even when there is some conflict with sons-in-law.

It is expected that homosexuality may cause ambivalence in relationships between gay and lesbian children and their parents because it is still seen as relatively uncommon and new. The embarrassment and disappointment parents feel when children do not create the assumed heterosexual family and the earlier conflict that occurs when "coming out of the closet" may create friction between parents and homosexual adult children. Alternatively, parents of gay and lesbian children may feel closer to them because of the difficulties they experience in life and because their relationships are not scripted by heterosexual expectations.

The relationships between *homosexual* adult children and their parents tend to be very positive, which was somewhat unexpected. However, both the parents and adult children were more likely than heterosexual children and parents to offer disclaimers or qualifications even when the relationship was positive. For example, adult children often said they were close to their parents but not as close as they had been before they disclosed their sexual orientation. The conflict that resulted when "coming out of the closet" was something that the sons and daughters said they could not forget. Likewise, parents were somewhat uncomfortable about their child's sexual orientation, even in good relationships. Parents and their homosexual children were also more likely to have estranged or displaced relationships, which was due to the parent's rejection of their child's homosexuality. Heterosexual children were very rarely estranged from parents and then only under extreme circumstances, such as in a case of sexual abuse in the family. Some of the adult children had occasional visits with parents even when parents did not approve of their homosexuality, but the visits were sporadic and riddled with contention. Because parents differed in their levels of acceptance among other things, homosexual couples often ended up spending more time with one spouse's family than the other spouse's family. Heterosexual couples were more likely to spend more time with the wife's family but still attempt to equalize time spent with each side of the family when all else was constant. Because of the tension between parents and their adult children and the child's desire to be "out" of the closet, some of the homosexual children moved far from their parents. Overall, there was a great deal of diversity between parents and homosexual adult children, suggesting the plurality of the homosexual experience. Relationships between parents and heterosexual children were more likely to be quite positive and fall within a narrower range.

There were also differences according to gender. Fathers had greater difficulty accepting a son who was gay than a daughter who was a lesbian. This may have been due to the continued effeminate stereotype that is linked to gay men but that is highly unacceptable in American society. Lesbian women and their lovers also tried harder to win their parents' acceptance than gay men. Mothers were more fearful of their child's safety and future than were fathers and were more concerned about what family and family friends would think of their child's sexuality. Parents and homosexual adult children were more likely to have a good relationship if they were close prior to the child coming out of the closet, suggesting the importance of earlier family patterns of problem solving, acceptance, and adaptation. Parents and homosexual children were also more inclined to have a close relationship if the parents were younger, suggesting generational differences in the acceptance of homosexuality.

THE EFFECT OF MARRIAGE ON PARENT–ADULT CHILD RELATIONSHIPS

Marriage had a profound effect on parent–adult child relationships for all of the adult children, but the effects differed by sexual orientation. Gay men and lesbians said the assumed permanence of marriage made a difference to their parents and resulted in their parents' greater acceptance of their relationship. Marriage meant something to their parents, causing them to see the relationship more positively. It was during the planning of the wedding that parents, sometimes for the first time, saw the extent to which their child's partner loved their child, also causing them to be favorably disposed to the new son-in-law or daughter-in-law. Parents were relieved that their child had found a lifelong partner. They had often been concerned that their child would have to remain single given the limited number of homosexuals and thus potential partners. In addition, the fact that marriage was an option for their homosexual child connoted an acceptance of their child's sexual orientation by the state, while attendance at the wedding implied consent by the greater family. All of these factors helped to make the relationship more normative and acceptable for parents and increased the likelihood of seeing their child's marriage within a spectrum of desirable life-course markers for adult children.

Many of these factors were less important for the parents of *heterosexual* children. Only one of the parents of a heterosexual child was concerned that her son's marriage would make the relationship public. This mother believed her daughter-in-law's lower educational level and social status made her an unacceptable spouse for her son. The parents of heterosexual adults were also more confident that their child would find a lifelong mate and so were not necessarily relieved by their marriage. The fact that their children were marrying was meaningful though for some parents if they did not like their child "living together" with a partner. Marriage thus decreased conflict for these parents and adult children.

A marriage and wedding could also have a negative effect on parent–adult child relationships. The wedding was difficult for parents who had not yet "gone public" with the news of their child's homosexuality to family or family friends. These parents were angry that their child's wedding would force them to do so. One parent yelled, "No! You cannot get married until after I am dead." The children of such parents were also angry with their mothers or fathers for being embarrassed by their sexuality. Some of the children saw how differently their parents handled their wedding versus a sibling's wedding, which was more of a celebratory occasion. Some of the gay and lesbian children realized that their parents did not invite colleagues and family friends to their weddings as they had to their siblings' weddings. These factors created ill will or conflict in the parent–adult child relationship.

The child's gender and the in-law's gender also made a difference in inter-generational relationships, but the effect of gender differed for heterosexual versus homosexual marriages. The mothers of *heterosexual sons* often felt they "lost" their son or that their son stepped back from his relationship with his birth family following marriage. These sons believed they had to focus on providing for their own families once they were married. In addition, they were often "pulled into" their wife's family after marriage due to women's greater likelihood of staying close to parents across the life course and the fact that the wives were the ones who set the couple's social calendar. Sons sometimes felt conflicted when their parents did not get along well with their wives. This resulted in them being less likely to visit parents and, in some cases, led to estrangement between parents and son. Even when there was no conflict, heterosexual sons were less likely to visit parents for an extended period of time without their wives. This was due to the higher level of mutual dependence and the specialization of tasks in heterosexual marriages. Gay sons, in contrast, felt less conflicted in visiting their parents. They were free to leave their husbands on their own due to their greater independence and the fact that they could (and did) equally perform all tasks. Thus, it was the way that we have defined heterosexual marriage and the husband versus wife role that led to conflict between heterosexual sons and their parents. In contrast, same-sex marriage provides a clean slate on which to rewrite the roles of same-sex partners anew rather than replicating the predominant institution of heterosexual marriage and its gender-based division of labor.

The characteristics attributed to femininity also improved the relationship between parents and their daughter's wife. Parents expected to be closer to their daughter's wife than to a son-in-law because of the presumed greater closeness to female relatives. Likewise, lesbian spouses often tried harder to get to know their new parents-in-law relative to sons-in-law. These factors led to parents saying they felt closer to their lesbian daughters-in-law than their heterosexual sons-in-law. In contrast to their daughter's wife, mothers sometimes felt they were in competition with their son's wife to retain control of their own families. This was because daughters stayed close to parents whether they were married to men or to women, while men's relationships with their parents were somewhat buffeted by their wives.

Estranged relationships between parents and homosexual adult children sometimes remained estranged even following marriage. Adult children were angry when their parents were not able to overcome their differences in order to attend their weddings. Rarely though did parents choose not to attend their child's wedding. However, some children did not invite their parents to their weddings if the parents had not been supportive previously.

There were a number of factors that increased the likelihood of marriage having a positive effect on parent–adult child relationships. Parents were more likely to respond to their child's wedding and marriage if the child "came out of the closet" earlier in life, thus increasing the length of time that the parents had to get used to their child's homosexuality. Parents also responded more positively to their child's same-sex marriage if they were able to separate out their feelings about homosexuality from their child. Finally, parents were more positive if they described their child's earlier years as troubled due to their sexuality. These parents were thus more appreciative that all had worked out for their child and that they had found a loving spouse.

These results highlight the importance of gender roles in parent-child relationships when there is a different sexual orientation. The predominant nature of gender roles in our society is so strong that they determine the quality and nature of parent-and-child relationships even in new social situations such as same-sex marriage. Parents and adult children are able to establish somewhat different relationships when there is a same-sex marriage though, suggesting that homosexual marriages are not completely replicating heterosexual marriages. The assumption of heterosexuality in our society is not so great that it reproduces new forms of marriage.

Most gay men and lesbians were close to their parents despite the suggestion in the literature that they receive less support than their heterosexual counterparts.[1] Relationships were less ambivalent when parents saw their child's marriage as falling within a range of what is regarded as acceptable and when their child was meeting other expected life-course markers, such as being employed. This highlights though the importance to parents of their children meeting expected life markers.[2] Since lesbians are more likely to raise children than are gay men, it may be that parents will experience less ambivalence with homosexual daughters versus sons. Indeed, fathers profess better relationships with lesbian daughters than gay sons. In addition, following marriage, parents see that their homosexual children are not as different from their heterosexual siblings as they had previously thought.

THE CONTOURS OF SAME-SEX MARRIAGE: IS SAME-SEX MARRIAGE CHANGING THE INSTITUTION OF MARRIAGE?

Critics of traditional marriage intended that the introduction of same-sex marriage would change the nature of marriage to such an extent that it would eliminate the unequal division of labor and power found in heterosexual marriage. These critics argued that the continued reinforcement of gender differentiation in heterosexual marriage creates our current cultural ideals of marriage and re-creates inequality.[3] Indeed, there is less gender differentiation in homosexual marriage and greater equality. Thus, to some extent, same-sex marriage has changed the nature of marriage in America today. It can be further argued that same-sex marriage makes the institution of marriage less "greedy" by requiring less of its members.[4]

There is some evidence that same-sex marriage has changed the nature of the institution of marriage in other countries as well. In the Netherlands, same-sex couples reject the division of labor that exists among heterosexual couples as was found in this study. Gay men in the Netherlands, however, are not monogamous the way that heterosexual men are in Massachusetts.[5] Married gay men were nearly as likely to be monogamous as were heterosexual men.

New combinations of gender dynamics change family relationships. In particular, the effect of marriage on the parent–adult child relationship differs when there are different combinations of genders interplaying. Having your son married to another man versus a woman lessens the competition found between mothers-in-law and their children-in-law. This leads to better relationships between parents and their married homosexual sons. Likewise, having your daughter marry another woman versus man makes in-law relationships closer because of women's tendencies to maintain close family ties and parents' expectations of closeness to daughters. The opportunity to set new expectations of family relationships following this recent type of family structure also leads to fresh possibilities as does the lessened interdependence found in traditional heterosexual marriage. All of these factors lead to new parent-child and in-law relationships following marriage.

Many progressives have advocated for this move away from the assumption of heterosexuality in our society and all that goes with it and an acceptance of homosexuality as an equal and publicly known alternative. They argue for a greater awareness and acceptance of the homosexual experience and family. In contrast to this study, others argue that the ability of same-sex couples to marry has not disrupted the dominance of heterosexuality.[6] Still other critics contend that we only undermine the institution of marriage overall by displacing formerly core public understandings of it and instead offering an array of equal alternatives.[7]

Homosexual couples were much more likely to have an equal division of labor and power than were the heterosexual couples in this study. They emphasized spending time together and sharing tasks and household labor, especially the tasks involved in raising children. Only one of the lesbian couples had a parent staying at home full time. Both spouses worked in all of the other homosexual couples, thus eschewing the traditional division of labor of breadwinner versus homemaker. Heterosexual couples were much more likely to have one parent at home and to have an unequal division of labor and decision making. Each individual often pursued his or her own separate interests and their own separate household tasks. Specialization of labor was a hallmark of these heterosexual marriages, with husbands often having responsibility for yard work and fixing things around the house while wives provided more of the care for children and the home.

Same-sex couples divide the labor of the home to optimize spending time together and creating equity and equality. They share in tasks so that no one person has the bulk of responsibility for household chores or child-rearing. By sharing interests and the responsibilities of the family and home, they build a life that optimizes their unity. Same-sex marriage is thus the model for how all marriages can be and a solution for the decrease in time that today's couples spend together.[8] Same-sex marriage is not undermining marriage but is instead strengthening it to resist the other social forces that tend to weaken it. Same-sex marriage is not a "greedy" form of marriage that robs each partner of time spent with extended family or in the community. Instead, it encourages couples to still participate in those outside interests but to do so together.

Same-sex marriage changes the nature of parent-and-child and in-law relationships as well. Gay sons are less likely to step back from their natal families following marriage than is the case for heterosexual sons. Mothers cite less tension with their sons' husbands than with their sons' wives. They also feel more comfortable in their gay sons' homes than in their daughters-in-law's homes. The new configuration of gender dynamics avoids the competition that sometimes exists in mother-in-law and daughter-in-law relationships. Likewise, parents-in-law get along better with their children-in-law from same-sex marriages. This is due to the greater "freedom" that same-sex couples tend to enjoy when there is no interdependency based on a specialization of tasks. Gay men felt much freer to visit parents for an extended period without their spouses than did heterosexual men. This may be the result of homosexual couples having a "clean slate" on which to rewrite the expectations of same-sex marriage and the assumptions of its spousal roles versus replicating a set of expectations based on heterosexuality. Overall, same-sex couples do not function like heterosexual couples.

Unlike homosexual men in the Netherlands, gay men in the United States tend to practice monogamy similar to heterosexual men.[9] Likewise, homosexual couples marry for some of the same reasons as do heterosexuals, such as seeing it as the optimal setting for raising children. However, gay men and lesbians also wish to marry for political reasons such as furthering gay and lesbian interests and asserting their right to marry. Thus, while there is some overlap in same-sex and heterosexual couples, overall same-sex couples do not function like heterosexual couples. Living as a gay man or lesbian is a separate but an equal and publicly known alternative to the heterosexual experience and family. Same-sex marriage can be seen as not "undermining" the family but bolstering it by focusing on equality, equity, and the sharing of home and family.

"DOING FAMILY"

Couples with a different sexual orientation "do family" or perform its tasks and carry forth its mandates in ways that are similar to but also different from heterosexuals. Like heterosexuals, many choose to marry during a time period in which there are multiple alternative living arrangements for adults. Similar to heterosexuals, lesbians often choose to raise children while gay men tend not to do so. Lesbians, however, must undergo a long and arduous process of either adopting children or undergoing fertility treatment. Becoming a parent is therefore always a planned decision for homosexuals while it may be an unplanned, de facto outcome for heterosexuals. "Doing parenting" for lesbians often involves bringing in male role models and perhaps individuals of the same race as the child. Same-sex parents also focus on more nonauthoritarian methods of disciplining and raising children together.

"Doing marriage" among homosexual couples consists of greater sharing of responsibilities out of a desire to be together. Same-sex couples remain close to extended family but try to minimize differences between themselves and their heterosexual family members. However, they are more likely to have estranged relationships with parents due to the parents' lack of acceptance of their homosexuality. Lesbians are actually seen as more avail-able to provide care to parents because they do not have a husband at home who needs care and attention. In fact, several of the lesbians were currently caring for elderly parents. Thus, homosexual couples "do family" in ways that are similar to heterosexuals. However, there is still a unique set of expec-tations and experiences for homosexuals that are distinct from heterosexual couples. The diversity of these expectations also suggests the diversity of the overall homosexual experience.

THE NUANCES OF SAME-SEX MARRIAGE AND FAMILY SYSTEMS

Results of this research show how the family is a system where what happens to one individual affects everyone else within the system. "Coming out" to one's parents affected not only the parent–adult child relationship but also all of the relationships within the family. Relationships between the siblings were affected if parents did not want their other children to remain in contact with their gay or lesbian child. Bonds between a parent and *their* siblings were also affected if one did not support the gay or lesbian family member while the sibling did. Grandparents, by and large, were consistently support-ive of their grandchildren even if they did not support homosexuality overall.

Gay and lesbian adults remained in contact with extended family mem-bers for the most part. However, there were instances in which they severed communication with a family member. This was more likely the further the relative was from the inner nuclear circle and when the family member was homophobic. Other family members were supportive of this withdrawal when they were aware of the homophobic comments.

THE EFFECT OF SEXUAL ORIENTATION ON THE COUPLE

Being part of a same-sex marriage had an important effect on the couple's relationship. There was often a negative effect on the couple when parents did not support their child's homosexuality or when they did not treat the spouse as a member of the family or as the child's legitimate partner. Homophobia also made it difficult for the couple to express their relationship publicly. They were cautious even around those family members who were supportive to decrease any discomfort. In addition, they downplayed their differences from the rest of the family. The difficulty of adopting a child or going through fertility treatments only made the couple closer though in order to support one another. Having to define their own marital roles and to construct their own marriages allowed couples to have greater freedom to customize their own marriage and to share more of their household responsibilities, leisure activities, and time with their children.

ADDITIONAL CONTOURS OF SAME-SEX MARRIAGE

Same-sex couples face significant challenges, even with the legalization of marriage. Gay men and lesbians often experience an initial disappointment from parents and sometimes extended family members when they come out of the closet. Their marriages may not be as extravagant or joyful as those of their heterosexual siblings. Overall, they do not receive the same levels of familial or institutional support that heterosexuals receive. Even good relationships with parents are qualified as being not *as good* as they were before coming out of the closet. Likewise, the Catholic Church does not support same-sex marriage nor do many areas offer services specific to the homosexual community, such as marriage counseling for same-sex couples. Same-sex couples also face additional challenges in acquiring children, either through adoption or with fertility treatments/surrogacy. These are the key turning points in the family lives of gay men and lesbians in America today.

Gay men and lesbians tend to marry later in life relative to heterosexuals. This can be advantageous though as a greater age at marriage decreases the likelihood of divorce. One of the main reasons today's couples married later was the need to wait for the legalization of same-sex marriage across the nation. It remains to be seen whether or not same-sex couples will continue to marry later now there is a uniform legalization of all marriages. Likewise, it is yet to be determined whether same-sex marriages will be more or less likely to end in divorce. However, three of the couples had divorced and another couple was considering separation, suggesting that same-sex marriages are certainly not immune to divorce.

THE IMPORTANCE OF THE TOPIC

This topic and the results of the research are important for a number of reasons. First we need to consider the potential impact of same-sex marriage on the institution and its ramifications. Some pundits have argued that same-sex marriage undermines marriage overall since it no longer functions as the most prestigious of the possible living arrangements for adults. In reality, the principle effect is to make marriage no longer the exclusive right of heterosexuals but to make that right and its benefits accessible for the gay and lesbian population. While same-sex marriage has changed some aspects of marriage, it does not appear to have lessened it; instead, same-sex marriage has improved the institution by promoting egalitarian marriages, focusing on greater sharing of household tasks, child-rearing, and leisure activities, and permitting both spouses to be independent enough to pursue relationships with their parents on their own. In the long run, this improves the parent-and-child relationship as well as the in-law relationship. Same-sex marriage affords each spouse greater freedom and an opportunity to write anew the expectations of marriage, marital roles, and the homosexual experience.

This topic is also important because it allows us to deepen our understanding of an alternative sexual orientation and the family experience of the homosexual community at a time in which same-sex marriage is just being legalized. We are able to learn more about the homosexual experience and to dispel the myths about the lesbian and gay community that is increasingly visible and accepted in mainstream society. That is not to say that homophobia does not still exist. However, the assumption of heterosexuality and all that goes with it is being increasingly challenged by discussions such as this one. This book highlights the diversity of the homosexual circumstance. There is no one prototype for lesbian and gay communities but instead a vast array of experiences on multiple dimensions that challenge stereotyping.

This book confirms the continued overall positive relationships between parents and adult children, even when children do not conform to their parents' expectations. This is important given the overall significance of the parent-and-child relationship across the life course and its influence on well-being for both parent and child. Although some of the parents and children experienced prolonged estrangement because of the parents' rejection of their child's homosexuality, most were able to return to earlier positive relationships. Many of the family members though described some alteration from the earlier relationship due to the conflict that resulted when the children disclosed their homosexuality or at the point of their relationship becoming public knowledge with a wedding. As a result, there was increased ambiguity in the relationship. It did not, however, prevent many of the daughters from being caregivers for their parents and will not do so in the future due to the depths of filial obligation.

This research also highlights the importance of both the time period and life course when researching families. This study occurs at a time when same-sex marriage has become increasingly acknowledged and accepted but while there is still significant homophobia. As a result, it shows the inherent conflicts and irony affecting today's same-sex couples. In addition, it shows the importance of the life course and one's place within it when examining family events. Where one is located within the life course and the effect of one's generational standing have important implications for how families cope and adapt.

Whether the lack of institutional support and parental support undermine marriage will require a much longer longitudinal study. While some of the couples married without parental approval, the long-term implications for the marriage and for family resilience remain to be tested. Early results though show that couples persevere in their desire to be together with or without family support and overall lack of institutional support.

Parent–adult child relationships are predominantly positive.[10] This remains the case even when the relationship is challenged by unexpected behavior from the adult child, such as marrying someone of the same sex. However, the relationship is also an ambivalent one, characterized by both positive and negative regard. Ambivalence is often manifested during status transitions, such as at the point of marriage.[11] In addition, intergenerational relations are also highly affected by the gender of the individuals and the combinations thereof.

The gay and lesbian community is both unique and diverse. Lesbians are more likely to have children than gay men, and they are more likely to marry.[12] Likewise, same-sex couples value equality more and experience more family functioning and less conflict than do heterosexual couples.[13] However, unlike earlier research, I find that gay men are nearly as likely to be monogamous as are heterosexuals and lesbians.[14]

THE FUTURE OF MARRIAGE IN AMERICA

The institution of marriage in America has undergone significant change over time. Prior to the seventeenth century, marriage was based on families allying themselves for political and economic reasons. From the seventeenth century onward, the emphasis on individual rights over patriarchal authority resulted in love-based marriage. Marriage became both more fragile and more optional since families no longer had any stake in supporting the marriages and adults expected love in their unions.[15] Since then, marriage has been further transformed from being focused on the raising of children and the importance of the nuclear family to being a source of personal fulfillment.[16] This change is seen as one of the main reasons for the high rate of divorce in America since people are free to divorce if they are no longer fulfilled. Marriage today is criticized for being both short lived and frequently entered into, referred to as the "marriage-go-round."[17] It is also criticized for benefiting men over women as a result of women's assumed subordinate role in marriage, women's greater responsibility for childcare and household management, and the priority given to the husband's job.

Progressives hope that same-sex marriage will change the institution of marriage. They would like to see marriage become less detrimental to women as a result of a greater emphasis on equity and equality. The results of this research suggest this in fact is the case. Same-sex marriages focus on a sharing of roles, household tasks and child-rearing, and leisure activities. Same-sex couples arrange their lives to be together rather than apart. They tend to be more egalitarian and to experience less conflict but higher family functioning. In this regard, same-sex couples have created marriages similar to those that the critics would like to see for heterosexual marriages. To the extent that heterosexuals look at the benefits accruing to the homosexual community, they may wish to change their own marriages to be more similar.

Likewise, the homosexual community is rewriting the expectations of relationships with parents and extended kin following marriage. Same-sex couples experience greater freedom in their marriages due to less of a division of gender-based roles between husband and wife. Results suggest this has the effect of improving relationships between adult children and their parents and between in-laws. Same-sex marriage then also improves intergenerational ties.

Now that same-sex marriage is legal in all fifty states, it will only serve to increase the acceptance and acknowledgment of same-sex marriage in America. The homosexual experience will be equal to the heterosexual one, making it possible for same-sex marriage to further influence all marriage. To this end, marriage may become the egalitarian institution that we would all like to experience with a greater sharing of family life and involvement in the community and possibly a decrease in the high rate of divorce today.

A FINAL NOTE TO PARENTS

In conclusion, parents will do well to remember that their child is still their child, whether gay/lesbian or heterosexual, and that they need you. In fact, your child will need you more as he or she navigates the complexities of same-sex marriage and bears the burden of a still-homophobic society. Separate your feelings about your child from your feelings about homosexuality and remember how much you have loved your child. He or she has not changed just because you now know about their sexual orientation. Be happy that your child has someone who loves him or her and can enjoy all of the privileges that come with marriage. Educate yourself about homosexuality and join a support group such as PFLAG, where you can meet other parents with similar experiences. Remember that your initial response to your child's disclosure of his or her homosexuality or announcement of their wedding will color the remainder of your relationship; thus measure your words. Above all else, remember that your child has turned to you for love and support, not for censure, and that you alone have the power to retain the relationship that you have always treasured.

Appendix
Methodology

THE DATA

This analysis is based on a comparison of two data sets. The first data set was collected for a previous study of married, heterosexual adult children and the mothers of such children.[1] This data set included interviews with twenty-five mothers who had at least one married son and one married daughter, and with twenty-five adult children who had been married for at least two years. The data were collected in and around 2009 in central New England.

The second data set was collected exclusively for this study. It incorporates a total of forty intensive interviews, including interviews with fifteen lesbian daughters who are or have been in a legal same-sex marriage, fifteen gay sons who are or have been in a legal same-sex marriage, and ten parents of at least one gay or lesbian adult child in a same-sex marriage and one adult child in a heterosexual marriage (for purposes of comparison). Thus, the adult children could be in a current same-sex marriage or divorced from a same-sex marriage. The latter were included to represent adult children whose same-sex marriages did not work out. There was one exception to this criterion though. The couple was getting married in another month, but their narrative was so rich in detail that they were included. All of the adult children also had to have one married heterosexual sibling for purposes of comparison. Again, there was one exception due to the richness of the data. Finally, all of the adult children had to have at least one parent alive at some point during their marriage to gauge the reaction of their parent to their marriage. There were two exceptions to this criterion. However, both of the women had been in long-term relationships with their partners while at least one parent was alive and permitted me to ask questions about the parent's reaction to their same-sex relationship, if not the marriage itself. One of the mothers interviewed was the parent of one of the lesbians who was also interviewed. This practice of interviewing the actual parent of the adult child was not continued, though, to increase the likelihood of both respondents truly volunteering and being honest when answering the questions. If only adult children who were willing to have a parent be interviewed had been selected, this would have skewed the data toward more positive relationships. Having one parent and adult child in the data set, however, did allow me to test for interrespondent validity.

The respondents for this second data set were recruited from several sources. Ads for respondents were placed in two newspapers, one free newspaper and one commercial newspaper. The ad included a statement of the purpose of the study: to interview adult children in same-sex marriages or parents of children in same-sex marriages about the relationship between the parent and adult child and how that has changed over time. It also included a statement that the respondent would be given a twenty-five-dollar honorarium, that the interviews would take place at the respondent's location of choice, and that the responses were confidential. I also attended meetings of PFLAG and asked for volunteers from those groups. Ads were also placed on the Facebook pages for the following local organizations: GLAAD (the Gay and Lesbian Alliance Against Defamation), local Pride groups, PFLAG (described above), and monoho (for gay men). Ads were also placed in local gay and lesbian clubs and bars. Finally, the leader of a gay/lesbian support group at a local large organization was contacted and asked to send an e-mail to all respondents describing and requesting participation in the study. Respondents were gathered from all five sources.

Interviews took place between May 2012 and December 2013. They lasted at least two hours and were usually recorded. I transcribed all of the interviews. Most took place in the respondent's home or a nearby public venue.

Results are not necessarily representative of the population. However, they can be instructive in explaining how relationships change after marriage in the homosexual population, the nature of same-sex marriage, and a comparison of how the effect of marriage on intergenerational relationships differs for heterosexuals versus homosexuals. Although this was not a randomly drawn population, it does include people from across all educational and income levels (including men and women who were unemployed and those who were on disability income). The data also include people with a wide array of intergenerational relationships and experiences and from a variety of ethnic backgrounds that represent the geographic area.

Qualitative data allow us to answer the questions presented in the literature and that is suggested by quantitative analysis. They allow us to answer questions about process, change, and the mechanisms through which family members create the patterns found in quantitative data. The strength of this particular data is that it is rich in information on how same-sex couples undergo change following marriage and that this change is described from the perspective of both adult children and parents. It is particularly important to talk to both generations given our focus on how marriage changes relationships with the adult child's family of orientation. For example, parents were much more expressive of their concerns for their children and how those concerns minimized any disruption to their own relationship with their child. A complete picture of the process by which changes unfold following marriage would not be possible without interviewing both parents and adult children. This data is also rich because it includes a newly legal form of marriage and thus tells us much about the institution of both marriage and same-sex coupling. It also examines an important point in intergenerational relationships and the process by which those relationships are changed.

DATA ANALYSIS

I transcribed all of the interviews to ensure data quality and maximum knowledge of the data. Content analysis was used. I recorded and categorized consistent themes that emerged from the data. This required a minimum of two readings of all of the transcripts, first to look for emerging themes and second to categorize the data. More often, however, three or more readings were required to categorize responses that were not obvious, that is, those that did not fit neatly into any one category.

MEASURES

Extent of Contact

Adult children were asked whether or not the couple sees more of their own relatives or their spouse's relatives, how often both the respondent and their spouse call their parents and in-laws, and whether each of them calls their own parents more than the spouse's parents. Not all children, nor all parents, were currently married, however. Adult children who were divorced were asked about the level of contact they and their spouse had with parents while they were married. Adult children whose parents were divorced were asked about separate contact with each parent. Those whose parents or in-laws were deceased were asked about contact on average before the parents' death. If the level of contact had changed because of an illness, contact both before and after the illness were recorded. Both measures were recorded if respondents differentiated contact with their mothers versus their fathers.

"Losing" One's Son or Daughter

Parents of adult children were also interviewed. They were asked whether or not they felt they had "lost" their sons or daughters when they married. I explained that this included the child stepping back from the natal family after marriage, cutting off ties, or otherwise disengaging from the natal family. I also asked mothers and fathers how their relationship with the child changed after marriage, if at all. The parents sometimes responded that this change was a matter of degree. I then categorized the cases according to the extent of change. Those cases in which the child called less after marriage or visited less, but still acted as part of the family, were counted as the parent not "losing" the child. Only those parents who described disengagement, significant change, or loss were categorized as having "lost" their son or daughter. Parents were also asked to describe what they did to maintain contact with their adult children after marriage.

Adult children were asked whether or not they felt they had "stepped back" from their natal families when they married, become less a part of the family, or disengaged from the family. Again, cases were categorized according to degree and were based on key words used by the respondent.

Notes

CHAPTER 1

1. Vern Bengtson, Timothy Biblarz, and Robert Roberts, *How Families Still Matter: A Longitudinal Study of Youth in Two Generations* (New York: Cambridge University Press, 2002); Ingrid Arnet Connidis, *Family Ties and Aging* (Los Angeles: Pine Forge Press, 2010); Karen L. Fingerman, *Aging Mothers and Their Adult Daughters: A Study in Mixed Emotions* (New York: Springer, 2001); Daphna Gans and Merril Silverstein, "Norms of Filial Responsibility for Aging Parents across Time and Generations," *Journal of Marriage and Family* 68, no. 4 (2006): 961–76; John R. Logan and Glenna D. Spitze, *Family Ties: Enduring Relations between Parents and Their Grown Children* (Philadelphia: Temple University Press, 1996); Christine M. Proulx and Heather M. Helms, "Mothers' and Fathers' Perception of Change and Continuity in Their Relationships with Young Adult Sons and Daughters," *Journal of Family Issues* 29, no. 2 (2008): 234–61; Alice Rossi and Peter Rossi, *Of Human Bonding: Parent-Child Relations across the Life Course* (New York: Aldine de Gruyter, 1990); J. Jill Suitor and Karl Pillemer, "Choosing Daughters: Exploring Why Mothers Favor Adult Daughters over Sons," *Sociological Perspectives* 49, no. 2 (2006): 221–30; Arland Thornton, Terri L. Orbuch, and William G. Axinn, "Parent-Child Relations during the Transition to Adulthood," *Journal of Family Issues* 16 (1995): 538–64.

2. Debra Umberson, "Relationships between Adult Children and Their Parents: Psychological Consequences for Both Generations," *Journal of Marriage and Family* 54 (1992): 664–74.

3. Connidis, *Family Ties*; Deborah M. Merrill, *When Your Children Marry: How Marriage Changes Relationships with Sons and Daughters* (Lanham, MD: Rowman & Littlefield, 2011).

4. Karen L. Fingerman, Elizabeth Hay, and Kira S. Birditt, "The Best of Ties, the Worst of Ties: Close, Problematic, and Ambivalent Social Relationships," *Journal of Marriage and Family* 66 (2004): 792–808.

5. Karl Pillemer and J. Jill Suitor, "Exploring Mothers' Ambivalence toward Their Adult Children," *Journal of Marriage and Family* 64 (2002): 601–13.

6. Rossi and Rossi, *Of Human Bonding*.

7. Diane Lye, "Adult Child-Parent Relationships," *Annual Review of Sociology* 22 (1996): 79–102; Leroy O. Stone, Carolyn J. Rosenthal, and Ingrid Arnet Connidis, *Parent-Child Exchanges of Support and Intergenerational Equity* (Ottawa, Canada: Statistics Canada, 1998).

8. Connidis, *Family Ties*.

9. Marilyn Coleman, Lawrence H. Ganong, and Tanya C. Rothrauff, "Racial and Ethnic Similarities and Differences in Beliefs About Intergenerational Assistance to Older Adults after Divorce and Remarriage," *Family Relations* 55 (2006): 576–87.

10. Ann Goetting, "Patterns of Support among In-Laws in the United States," *Journal of Family Issues* 11, no. 1 (1990): 67–90; Eunju Lee, Glenna Spitze, and John R. Logan, "Social Support to Parents-in-Law: The Interplay of Gender and Kin Hierarchies," *Journal of Marriage and Family* 65 (2003): 396–403; Kim Shuey and Melissa Hardy, "Assistance to Aging Parents and Parents-in-Law: Does Lineage Affect Family Allocation Decisions?" *Journal of Marriage and Family* 65 (2003): 418–31.

11. Rossi and Rossi, *Of Human Bonding*.

12. Andrea E. Willson, Kim M. Shuey, and Glenn H. Elder Jr., "Ambivalence in the Relationships of Adult Children to Aging Parents and In-Laws," *Journal of Marriage and Family* 65 (2003): 1055–72.

13. Pillemer and Suitor, "Exploring Mothers' Ambivalence."

14. Deborah M. Merrill, *Caring for Elderly Parents: Juggling Work, Family, and Caregiving in Middle and Working Class Families* (Westport, CT: Auburn House, 1997).

15. Lynn White, "The Effect of Parental Divorce and Remarriage on Parental Support of Adult Children," *Journal of Family Issues* 13, no. 2 (1992): 234–50.

16. Janet Finch and Jennifer Mason, *Passing On: Kinship and Inheritance in England* (New York: Routledge, 2000).

17. Natalia Sarkisian and Naomi Gerstel, "Till Marriage Do Us Part: Adult Children's Relationships with Their Parents," *Journal of Marriage and Family* 70 (2008): 360–76.

18. Merrill, *When Your Children Marry*.

19. Umberson, "Relationships."

20. Lawrence Kurdek, "Are Gay and Lesbian Cohabiting Couples *Really* Different from Heterosexual Married Couples?" *Journal of Marriage and Family* 66 (November 2004): 880–900; Lawrence Kurdek, "Differences between Partners from Heterosexual, Gay, and Lesbian Cohabiting Couples," *Journal of Marriage and Family* 68 (May 2006): 509–28.

21. Y. Elizer and A. Mintzer, "Gay Males' Intimate Relationship Quality: The Roles of Attachment Security, Gay Identity, Social Support, and Income," *Personal Relationships* 10 (2003): 411–35.

22. Anonymous, "Like Her Own: Ideals and Experiences of the Mother-in-Law and Daughter-in-Law Relationship," *Journal of Family Issues* submission (2014);

Deborah M. Merrill, *Mothers-in-Law and Daughters-in-Law: Understanding the Relationship and What Makes Them Friends or Foe* (Westport, CT: Praeger, 2007).

23. Drew DeSilver, "How Many Same-Sex Marriages in the U.S.?" Pew Research Center, FACTANK, June 26, 2013. Accessed June 20, 2015. http://www.pewresearch.org/.

24. Mark Sherman, "Supreme Court Ruling a Big Win for Gay Marriage," *Worcester (MA) Telegram and Gazette*, October 7, 2014, A9.

25. Drew DeSilver, "A Global Snapshot of Same-Sex Marriage." Pew Research Center, FACTANK, June 4, 2013. Accessed June 20, 2015. http://www.pew research.org/.

26. G. Gates, *New Census Bureau Data Show Annual Increases in Same-Sex Couples Outpacing Population Growth: Same-Sex Couples Affected by Recession* (Los Angeles: Williams Institute, UCLA School of Law, 2010).

27. G. Gates, M. Badgett, and D. Ho. *Marriage, Registration, and Dissolution by Same-Sex Couples in the U.S.* (Los Angeles: Williams Institute, UCLA School of Law, 2008).

28. M. V. Lee Badgett, *When Gay People Get Married* (New York: New York University Press, 2009).

29. G. Gates, *Same-Sex Spouses and Unmarried Partners in the American Community Survey, 2008* (Los Angeles: Williams Institute, UCLA School of Law, 2009).

30. T. Simmons and M. O'Connell, "Married-Couple and Unmarried-Partner Households: 2000," *Census 2000 Special Report*, February 2003.

31. Gates, *New Census Bureau Data.*

32. Gates, *Same-Sex Spouses.*

33. Brad van Eeden-Moorefield, Christopher R. Martell, Mark Williams, and Marilyn Preston, "Same-Sex Relationships and Dissolution: The Connection Between Heteronormativity and Homonormativity," *Family Relations* 60 (December 2011): 562–71.

34. Elizer and Mintzer, "Gay Males' Intimate."

35. Sharon S. Rostosky, Ellen D. B. Riggle, Todd A. Savage, Staci D. Roberts, and Gilbert Singletary, "Interracial Same-Sex Couples' Perceptions of Stress and Coping: An Exploratory Study," *Journal of GLBT Family Studies* 4, no. 3 (2008): 277–99.

36. Liza Mundy, "The Gay Guide to Wedded Bliss," *Atlantic*, June 2013, 56–66, 68, 70.

37. Michael Rosenfeld, "Couple Longevity in the Era of Same-Sex Marriage in the United States," *Journal of Marriage and Family* 76, no. 5 (October 2014): 905–18.

38. Kurdek, "Are Gay and Lesbian?"

39. Kurdek, "Differences between Partners"; Mundy, "Gay Guide."

40. Badgett, *When Gay People.*

41. Rachel Farr and Charlotte J. Patterson, "Coparenting among Lesbian, Gay, and Heterosexual Couples: Associations with Adopted Children's Outcomes," *Child Development* 84, no. 4 (July–August 2013): 1226–40.

42. Lon B. Johnston, Brenda A. Moore, and Rebecca Judd, "Gay and Lesbian Households' Perceptions of Their Family Functioning: Strengths and Resiliency," *Journal of GLBT Family Studies* 6, no. 3 (2010): 315–25.

43. Kurdek, "Differences between Partners."

44. Badgett, *When Gay People*; Thomas S. Dee, "Forsaking All Others? The Effects of 'Gay Marriage' on Risky Sex," *Economic Journal* 118 (July 2008): 1055–78.

45. Peter Robinson, *Gay Men's Relationships across the Life Course* (London: Palgrave Macmillan, 2013).

46. Merrill, *When Your Children Marry*.

47. Badgett, *When Gay People*.

48. Elizer and Mintzer, "Gay Males' Intimate"; Kurdek, "Differences between Partners"; Sondra E. Solomon, Esther D. Rothblum, and Kimberly F. Balsam, "Money, Housework, Sex, and Conflict: Same-Sex Couples in Civil Unions, Those Not in Civil Unions, and Heterosexual Married Siblings," *Sex Roles* 52 (May 2005): 561–75.

49. As an example, see Sarah F. Pearlman, *Mother-Talk Conversations with Mothers of Lesbian Daughters and FTM Transgender Children* (Toronto: Demeter, 2012).

50. Esther D. Rothblum, "Mars to Venus or Earth to Earth? How Do Families of Origin Fit into GLBTQ Lives?" *Journal of GLBT Family Studies* 10, nos. 1–2 (2014): 231–41.

51. Colleen M. Connolly, "A Process of Change: The Intersection of the GLBT Individual and Their Family of Origin," *Journal of GLBT Family Studies* 1, no. 1 (2005): 5–20.

52. Theresa Reeves, Sharon G. Horne, Sharon Scales Rostosky, Ellen D. B. Riggle, Linda R. Baggett, and Rebecca A. Aycock, "Family Members' Support for GLBT Issues: The Role of Family Adaptability and Cohesion," *Journal of GLBT Family Studies* 6, no. 1 (2010): 80–97.

53. Merrill, *Mothers-in-Law*.

54. Sarkisian and Gerstel, "Till Marriage Do Us Part."

55. Karen Loscoco and Susan Walzer, "Gender and the Culture of Heterosexual Marriage in the United States," *Journal of Family Theory and Review* 5 (March 2013): 1–14.

56. Chiara Bertone and Marina Franchi, "Suffering as the Path to Acceptance: Parents of Gay and Lesbian Young People Negotiating Catholicism in Italy," *Journal of GLBT Family Studies* 10, no. 1 (2014): 58–78.

57. Maggie Gallagher, "(How) Will Gay Marriage Weaken Marriage as a Social Institution? A Reply to Andrew Koppelmann," *University of St. Thomas Law Review* 2 (2004): 33–70.

58. Badgett, *When Gay People*.

59. Balsam, Rothblum, and Solomon, "Narratives of Same-Sex Couples"; Balsam, Rothblum, and Solomon, "Longest 'Legal'"; Kurdek, "Differences between Partners"; Mundy, "Gay Guide."

60. van Eeden-Moorefield et al., "Same-Sex Relationships."

61. Merrill, *When Your Children Marry*.

CHAPTER 2

1. Rothblum, "Mars to Venus."
2. Chiara Bertone and Maria Pallotta-Chiarolli, "Putting Families of Origin into the Queer Picture: Introducing This Special Issue," *Journal of GLBT Family Studies* 10, nos. 1–2 (2014): 1–14.
3. Rothblum, "Mars to Venus"; Janet B. Watson, "Bisexuality and Family: Narratives of Silence, Solace, and Strength," *Journal of GLBT Family Studies* 10, nos. 1–2 (2014): 101–23.
4. Connolly, "Process of Change."
5. Watson, "Bisexuality and Family."
6. Alenka Svab and Roman Kuhar, "The Transparent and Family Closets: Gay Men and Lesbians and Their Families of Origin," *Journal of GLBT Family Studies* 10, no. 1 (2014): 15–35.
7. Bertone and Pallotta-Chiarolli, "Putting Families."
8. Connolly, "Process of Change."
9. Erika L. Grafsky, "Becoming the Parent of a GLB Son or Daughter," *Journal of GLBT Family Studies* 10, no. 1 (2014): 36–57.
10. Ibid.
11. Karl Pillemer and J. Jill Suitor, "Exploring Mothers' Ambivalence toward Their Adult Children," *Journal of Marriage and Family* 64 (2002): 601–13.
12. Rothblum, "Mars to Venus."

CHAPTER 3

1. Merrill, *When Your Children Marry.*
2. Vern L. Bengtson, Roseann Giarusso, J. Beth Mabry, and Merril Silverstein, "Solidarity, Conflict, and Ambivalence: Complementary or Competing Perspectives on Intergenerational Relationships?" *Journal of Marriage and Family* 64, no. 3 (2002): 568–76; Connidis, *Family Ties.*
3. Merrill, *When Your Children Marry.*
4. Goetting, "Patterns of Support"; Lee, Spitze, and Logan, "Social Support"; Shuey and Hardy, "Assistance to Aging Parents."
5. Merrill, *When Your Children Marry.*
6. Ibid.
7. Umberson, "Relationships."
8. This is not to suggest that parents of heterosexual children liked all of their children-in-law. However, situations where parents did not like their child's spouse were not among the best of the heterosexual child–parent relationships.
9. Merrill, *When Your Children Marry.*
10. Carol Gilligan, *In a Different Voice: Psychological Theory and Women's Development* (Cambridge, MA: Harvard University Press, 1982).
11. Badgett, *When Gay People.*

CHAPTER 4

1. For a comprehensive review, see Connidis, *Family Ties*.
2. Pillemer and Suitor, "Exploring Mothers' Ambivalence."
3. Sarkisian and Gerstel, "Till Marriage Do Us Part."
4. Merrill, *When Your Children Marry*.
5. Ibid.
6. Merrill, *Mothers-in-Law*.
7. Sarkisian and Gerstel, "Till Marriage Do Us Part."
8. Merrill, *When Your Children Marry*.
9. Ibid.
10. Paul R. Amato, Alan Booth, David R. Johnson, and Stacy J. Rogers, *Alone Together: How Marriage in America Is Changing* (Cambridge, MA: Harvard University Press, 2007).

CHAPTER 5

1. D'Vera Cohn, Jeffrey S. Passel, Wendy Wang, and Gretchen Livingston, "Barely Half of U.S. Adults Are Married—A Record Low," Pew Research Center, Social and Demographic Trends, December 14, 2011, accessed May 28, 2015, http://www.pew-socialtrends.org/; Mark Mather and Diana Lavery, "In U.S., Proportion Married at Lowest Recorded Levels," Population Reference Bureau Publications, 2010, accessed May 28, 2015, http://www.pbr.org/; Wendy Wang, "Record Share of Americans Have Never Married," Pew Research Center, Social and Demographic Trends, September 24, 2014, accessed May 28, 2015, http://www.pewsocialtrends.org/.
2. Wang, "Record Share."
3. Ibid.
4. Andrew Cherlin, *The Marriage-Go-Round: The State of Marriage and the Family in America Today* (New York: Knopf, 2009).
5. Elizabeth A. Sharp and Lawrence Ganong, "I'm a Loser, I'm Not Married, Let's Just All Look at Me," *Journal of Family Issues* 32, no. 7 (July 2011): 956–80.
6. Maria J. Kefalas, Frank Furstenberg, Patrick J. Carr, and Laura Napolitano, "Marriage Is More than Being Together," *Journal of Family Issues* 32, no. 7 (July 2011): 845–75.
7. Ibid.
8. Badgett, *When Gay People*, 89.
9. Ibid., 99.
10. CDC/NCHS National Vital Statistics Report, quoted in Paula J. Owen, "'No Money,' No Marriage? These Days, Finances Are Often to Blame for Couples Deciding to Not Get Hitched," *Worcester (MA) Telegram and Gazette*, July 21, 2014.
11. Wang, "Record Share."

12. Suzanne M. Bianchi, John P. Robinson, and Melissa A. Milkie, *Changing Rhythms of American Family Life* (New York: Russell Sage Foundation, 2007).

13. Badgett, *When Gay People*; Kurdek, "Differences between Partners."

14. Judith Stacey, "Gay and Lesbian Families: Queer Like Us," in *Family in Transition*, ed. Arlene S. Skolnick and Jerome H. Skolnick, 496–518 (Boston: Pearson Allyn & Bacon, 2011).

15. Badgett, *When Gay People*.

16. Amato et al., *Alone Together*.

CHAPTER 6

1. Gary Gates, *LGB Families and Relationships: Analyses of the 2013 National Health Interview Survey* (Los Angeles: Williams Institute, UCLA School of Law, 2014).

2. Stacey, "Gay and Lesbian Families."

3. About.com, "Fertility," accessed August 18, 2014, http://www.infertility.about.com/.

4. Reproductive Technologies, Sperm Bank of California, accessed August 18, 2014, http://www.thespermbankofca.org/.

5. "Intrauterine Insemination (IUI)," American Society for Reproductive Medicine, last updated 2012, accessed July 1, 2015, https://www.asrm.org/.

6. "State Adoption Laws," Human Rights Campaign, accessed August 18, 2014, http://www.hrc.org/; Life Long Adoptions, accessed August 18, 2014, http://www.lifelongadoptions.com/.

7. "Family Law," Find Law, accessed August 18, 2014, http://family.findlaw.com/.

8. Judith Stacey and Timothy J. Biblarz, "(How) Does the Sexual Orientation of Parents Matter?" *American Sociological Review* 66 (2001): 159–83; Stacey, "Gay and Lesbian Families."

9. Abbie E. Goldberg, "Gay- and Lesbian-Parent Families: Functioning and Development in Context," in *Families and Change: Coping with Stressful Life Events and Transitions*, ed. S. Price, C. Price, and P. C. McHenry, 263–84 (Thousand Oaks, CA: Sage, 2009); Abbie E. Goldberg and J. Z. Smith, "Stigmas, Social Context, and Mental Health: Lesbian and Gay Couples across the Transition to Adoptive Parenthood," *Journal of Counseling Psychology* 58, (2011): 139–50; Abbie E. Goldberg, *Gay Dads: Transitions to Adoptive Parenthood* (New York: New York University Press, 2012); L. A. Kinkler and A. E. Goldberg, "Working with What We've Got: Perception of Barriers and Support among Same-Sex Adopting Couples in Non-Metropolitan Areas," *Family Relations* 60 (2011): 387–403.

10. Many of the couples adopted before both same-sex marriage and second-parent adoption were possible.

CHAPTER 7

1. Badgett, *When Gay People*; Kurdek, "Are Gay and Lesbian?"; Kurdek, "Differences between Partners"; van Eeden-Moorefield et al., "Same-Sex Relationships."

2. Badgett, *When Gay People*.

3. Dee, "Forsaking All Others?"

4. Kurdek, "Are Gay and Lesbian?"; Solomon, Rothblum, and Balsam, "Money, Housework."

5. Mundy, "Gay Guide."

6. U.S. Bureau of Labor Statistics, "Marriage and Divorce: Patterns by Gender, Race, and Educational Attainment," *Monthly Labor Review* (October 2013): 1–19.

7. Badgett, *When Gay People*; Mundy, "Gay Guide."

8. Julie L. Shulman, Gabrielle Gotta, and Robert-Jay Green, "Will Marriage Matter? Effects of Marriage Anticipated by Same-Sex Couples," *Journal of Family Issues* 33, no. 2 (2012): 158–81.

9. Bob was in his early sixties at the time of the interview. It was not clear whether his workmates were as homophobic as he suggested or whether he was reflecting attitudes from an earlier point in time.

10. Badgett, *When Gay People*; Robinson, *Gay Men's Relationships*.

11. Badgett, *When Gay People*.

12. Balsam, Rothblum, and Solomon, "Narratives of Same-Sex Couples"; Balsam, Rothblum, and Solomon, "Longest 'Legal'"; Farr and Patterson, "Coparenting"; Mundy, "Gay Guide."

CHAPTER 8

1. Bertone and Pallotta-Chiarolli, "Putting Families"; Valeria Cappellato and Tiziana Mangarella, "Sexual Citizenship in Private and Public Space: Parents of Gay Men and Lesbians Discuss Their Experiences of Pride Parades," *Journal of GLBT Family Studies* 10, nos. 1–2 (2014): 211–30; Grafsky, "Becoming the Parent"; Pearlman, *Mother-Talk Conversations*; Reeves et al., "Family Members' Support."

2. Connolly, "Process of Change"; Watson, "Bisexuality and Family."

3. Connidis, *Family Ties*.

4. Valerie Q. Glass, "We Are Family: Black Lesbian Couples Negotiate Rituals with Extended Families," *Journal of GLBT Family Studies* 10, nos. 1–2 (2014): 79–100.

5. Shelly Smith-Acuna, *Systems Theory in Action: Applications to Individual, Couple, and Family Therapy* (Hoboken, NJ: Wiley).

6. Ibid.

7. Bertone and Pallotta-Chiarolli, "Putting Families."

CHAPTER 9

1. Gates, *New Census Bureau Data.*
2. Merrill, *Caring for Elderly Parents.*
3. Lesbians, gay men, and transsexuals often attend the PFLAG meetings as well as the family members of such groups.

CHAPTER 10

1. Elizer and Mintzer, "Gay Males' Intimate"; Kurdek, "Differences between Partners"; Solomon, Rothblum, and Balsam, "Money, Housework."
2. Pillemer and Suitor, "Exploring Mothers' Ambivalence."
3. Sarkisian and Gerstel, "Till Marriage Do Us Part."
4. Ibid.
5. Badgett, *When Gay People.*
6. Katrina Kimport, *Queering Marriage: Challenging Family Formation in the United States* (New Brunswick, NJ: Rutgers University Press, 2014).
7. Gallagher, "(How) Will Gay Marriage?"
8. Amato et al., *Alone Together.*
9. Badgett, *When Gay People.*
10. See Connidis, *Family Ties,* for an overview.
11. Pillemer and Suitor, "Exploring Mothers' Ambivalence."
12. Gates, *Same-Sex Spouses.*
13. Johnston, Moore, and Judd, "Gay and Lesbian"; Balsam, Rothblum, and Solomon, "Longest 'Legal.'"
14. Badgett, *When Gay People.*
15. Stephanie Coontz, *Marriage: A History; How Love Conquered Marriage* (New York: Penguin, 2005).
16. Paul Amato, "Tension between Institutional and Individual Views of Marriage," *Journal of Marriage and Family* 66 (2004): 959–65; Amato et al., *Alone Together*; Andrew Cherlin, "The Deinstitutionalization of American Marriage," *Journal of Marriage and Family* 66 (November 2004): 848–61; Cherlin, *Marriage-Go-Round*; Coontz, *Marriage.*
17. Cherlin, *Marriage-Go-Round.*

APPENDIX

1. See Merrill, *When Your Children Marry.*

Bibliography

About.com. "Fertility." Accessed August 18, 2014. http://www.infertility.about.com/.

Allen, Katherine R. "Reflexivity in Qualitative Analysis: Toward an Understanding of Resiliency among Older Parents with Adult Gay Children." In *The Dynamics of Resilient Families*, edited by Hamilton I. McCubbin, Elizabeth A. Thompson, Anne I. Thompson, and Jo A. Futrell, 71–98. Thousand Oaks, CA: Sage Publications, 1999.

Amato, Paul. "Tension between Institutional and Individual Views of Marriage." *Journal of Marriage and Family* 66 (2004): 959–65.

Amato, Paul R., Alan Booth, David R. Johnson, and Stacy J. Rogers. *Alone Together: How Marriage in America Is Changing*. Cambridge, MA: Harvard University Press, 2007.

American Society for Reproductive Medicine. "Intrauterine Insemination (IUI)." Last updated 2012. Accessed July 1, 2015. https://www.asrm.org/.

Anonymous. "Like Her Own: Ideals and Experiences of the Mother-in-Law and Daughter-in-Law Relationship." *Journal of Family Issues* submission, 2014.

Badgett, M. V. Lee. *When Gay People Get Married*. New York: New York University Press, 2009.

Balsam, Kimberly F., Esther D. Rothblum, and Sondra E. Solomon. "The Longest 'Legal' U.S. Same-Sex Couples Reflect on Their Relationships." *Journal of Social Sciences* 67, no. 2 (June 2011): 302–15.

———. "Narratives of Same-Sex Couples Who Had Civil Unions in Vermont: The Impact of Legalizing Relationships on Couples and on Social Policy." *Sexuality Research and Social Policy* 8, no. 3 (September 2011): 183–91.

Bengtson, Vern, Timothy Biblarz, and Robert Roberts. *How Families Still Matter: A Longitudinal Study of Youth in Two Generations*. New York: Cambridge University Press, 2002.

Bengtson, Vern L., Roseann Giarusso, J. Beth Mabry, and Merril Silverstein. "Solidarity, Conflict, and Ambivalence: Complementary or Competing Perspectives on Intergenerational Relationships?" *Journal of Marriage and Family* 64, no. 3 (2002): 568–76.

Bertone, Chiara, and Marina Franchi. "Suffering as the Path to Acceptance: Parents of Gay and Lesbian Young People Negotiating Catholicism in Italy." *Journal of GLBT Family Studies* 10, no. 1 (2014): 58–78.

Bertone, Chiara, and Maria Pallotta-Chiarolli. "Putting Families of Origin into the Queer Picture: Introducing This Special Issue." *Journal of GLBT Family Studies* 10, nos. 1–2 (2014): 1–14.

Bianchi, Suzanne M., John P. Robinson, and Melissa A. Milkie. *Changing Rhythms of American Family Life*. New York: Russell Sage Foundation, 2007.

Cappellato, Valeria, and Tiziana Mangarella. "Sexual Citizenship in Private and Public Space: Parents of Gay Men and Lesbians Discuss Their Experiences of Pride Parades." *Journal of GLBT Family Studies* 10, nos. 1–2 (2014): 211–30.

Cherlin, Andrew. "The Deinstitutionalization of American Marriage." *Journal of Marriage and Family* 66 (November 2004): 848–61.

———. *The Marriage-Go-Round: The State of Marriage and the Family in America Today*. New York: Knopf, 2009.

Cohn, D'Vera, Jeffrey S. Passel, Wendy Wang, and Gretchen Livingston. "Barely Half of U.S. Adults Are Married—A Record Low." Pew Research Center, Social and Demographic Trends, December 14, 2011. Accessed May 28, 2015. http://www.pewsocialtrends.org/.

Coleman, Marilyn, Lawrence H. Ganong, and Tanya C. Rothrauff. "Racial and Ethnic Similarities and Differences in Beliefs About Intergenerational Assistance to Older Adults after Divorce and Remarriage." *Family Relations* 55 (2006): 576–87.

Connidis, Ingrid Arnet. *Family Ties and Aging*. Los Angeles: Pine Forge Press, 2010.

Connolly, Colleen M. "A Process of Change: The Intersection of the GLBT Individual and Their Family of Origin." *Journal of GLBT Family Studies* 1, no. 1 (2005): 5–20.

Coontz, Stephanie. *Marriage: A History; How Love Conquered Marriage*. New York: Penguin, 2005.

Dee, Thomas S. "Forsaking All Others? The Effects of 'Gay Marriage' on Risky Sex." *Economic Journal* 118 (July 2008): 1055–78.

DeSilver, Drew. "A Global Snapshot of Same-Sex Marriage." Pew Research Center, FACTANK, June 4, 2013. Accessed June 20, 2015. http://www.pewresearch.org/.

———. "How Many Same-Sex Marriages in the U.S.?" Pew Research Center, FACTANK, June 26, 2013. Accessed June 20, 2015. http://www.pewresearch.org/.

Elizer, Y., and A. Mintzer. "Gay Males' Intimate Relationship Quality: The Roles of Attachment Security, Gay Identity, Social Support, and Income." *Personal Relationships* 10 (2003): 411–35.

Farr, Rachel, and Charlotte J. Patterson. "Coparenting among Lesbian, Gay, and Heterosexual Couples: Associations with Adopted Children's Outcomes." *Child Development* 84, no. 4 (July–August 2013): 1226–40.

Finch, Janet, and Jennifer Mason. *Passing On: Kinship and Inheritance in England*. New York: Routledge, 2000.

Find Law. "Family Law." Accessed August 18, 2014. http://family.findlaw.com/.

Fingerman, Karen L. *Aging Mothers and Their Adult Daughters: A Study in Mixed Emotions.* New York: Springer, 2001.

Fingerman, Karen L., Elizabeth Hay, and Kira S. Birditt. "The Best of Ties, the Worst of Ties: Close, Problematic, and Ambivalent Social Relationships." *Journal of Marriage and Family* 66 (2004): 792–808.

Gallagher, Maggie. "(How) Will Gay Marriage Weaken Marriage as a Social Institution? A Reply to Andrew Koppelmann." *University of St. Thomas Law Review* 2 (2004): 33–70.

Gans, Daphna, and Merril Silverstein. "Norms of Filial Responsibility for Aging Parents across Time and Generations." *Journal of Marriage and Family* 68, no. 4 (2006): 961–76.

Gates, Gary. *LGB Families and Relationships: Analyses of the 2013 National Health Interview Survey.* Los Angeles: Williams Institute, UCLA School of Law, 2014.

———. *New Census Bureau Data Show Annual Increases in Same-Sex Couples Outpacing Population Growth: Same-Sex Couples Affected by Recession.* Los Angeles: Williams Institute, UCLA School of Law, 2010.

———. *Same-Sex Spouses and Unmarried Partners in the American Community Survey, 2008.* Los Angeles: Williams Institute, UCLA School of Law, 2009.

Gates, G., M. Badgett, and D. Ho. *Marriage, Registration, and Dissolution by Same-Sex Couples in the U.S.* Los Angeles: Williams Institute, UCLA School of Law, 2008.

Gilligan, Carol. *In a Different Voice: Psychological Theory and Women's Development.* Cambridge, MA: Harvard University Press, 1982.

Glass, Valerie Q. "We Are Family: Black Lesbian Couples Negotiate Rituals with Extended Families." *Journal of GLBT Family Studies* 10, nos. 1–2 (2014): 79–100.

Goetting, Ann. "Patterns of Support among In-Laws in the United States." *Journal of Family Issues* 11, no. 1 (1990): 67–90.

Goldberg, Abbie E. "Gay- and Lesbian-Parent Families: Functioning and Development in Context." In *Families and Change: Coping with Stressful Life Events and Transitions*, edited by S. Price, C. Price, and P. C. McHenry, 263–84. Thousand Oaks, CA: Sage, 2009.

———. *Gay Dads: Transitions to Adoptive Parenthood.* New York: New York University Press, 2012.

Goldberg, Abbie E., and J. Z. Smith. "Stigmas, Social Context, and Mental Health: Lesbian and Gay Couples across the Transition to Adoptive Parenthood." *Journal of Counseling Psychology* 58 (2011): 139–50.

Grafsky, Erika L. "Becoming the Parent of a GLB Son or Daughter." *Journal of GLBT Family Studies* 10, no. 1 (2014): 36–57.

Human Rights Campaign. "State Adoption Laws." Accessed August 18, 2014. http://www.hrc.org/.

Johnston, Lon B., Brenda A. Moore, and Rebecca Judd. "Gay and Lesbian Households' Perceptions of Their Family Functioning: Strengths and Resiliency." *Journal of GLBT Family Studies* 6, no. 3 (2010): 315–25.

Kefalas, Maria J., Frank Furstenberg, Patrick J. Carr, and Laura Napolitano. "Marriage Is More than Being Together." *Journal of Family Issues* 32, no 7 (July 2011): 845–75.

Kerr, Michael E., and Murray Bowen. *Family Evaluation: An Approach Based on Bowen Theory*. New York: Norton, 1988.

Kimport, Katrina. *Queering Marriage: Challenging Family Formation in the United States*. New Brunswick, NJ: Rutgers University Press, 2014.

Kinkler, L. A., and A. E. Goldberg. "Working with What We've Got: Perception of Barriers and Support among Same-Sex Adopting Couples in Non-Metropolitan Areas." *Family Relations* 60 (2011): 387–403.

Kurdek, Lawrence. "Are Gay and Lesbian Cohabiting Couples *Really* Different from Heterosexual Married Couples?" *Journal of Marriage and Family* 66 (November 2004): 880–900.

———. "Differences between Partners from Heterosexual, Gay, and Lesbian Cohabiting Couples." *Journal of Marriage and Family* 68 (May 2006): 509–28.

Lee, Eunju, Glenna Spitze, and John R. Logan. "Social Support to Parents-in-Law: The Interplay of Gender and Kin Hierarchies." *Journal of Marriage and Family* 65 (2003): 396–403.

Logan, John R., and Glenna D. Spitze. *Family Ties: Enduring Relations between Parents and Their Grown Children*. Philadelphia: Temple University Press, 1996.

Loscoco, Karen, and Susan Walzer. "Gender and the Culture of Heterosexual Marriage in the United States." *Journal of Family Theory and Review* 5 (March 2013): 1–14.

Lye, Diane. "Adult Child-Parent Relationships." *Annual Review of Sociology* 22 (1996): 79–102.

Mather, Mark, and Diana Lavery. "In U.S., Proportion Married at Lowest Record Levels." Population Reference Bureau Publications, 2010. Accessed May 28, 2015. http://www.pbr.org/.

Merrill, Deborah M. *Caring for Elderly Parents: Juggling Work, Family, and Caregiving in Middle and Working Class Families*. Westport, CT: Auburn House, 1997.

———. *Mothers-in-Law and Daughters-in-Law: Understanding the Relationship and What Makes Them Friends or Foe*. Westport, CT: Praeger, 2007.

———. *When Your Children Marry: How Marriage Changes Relationships with Sons and Daughters*. Lanham, MD: Rowman & Littlefield, 2011.

Mundy, Liza. "The Gay Guide to Wedded Bliss." *Atlantic*, June 2013, 56–66, 68, 70.

Owen, Paula J. "'No Money,' No Marriage? These Days, Finances Are Often to Blame for Couples Deciding to Not Get Hitched." *Worcester (MA) Telegram and Gazette*, July 21, 2014.

Pearlman, Sarah F. *Mother-Talk Conversations with Mothers of Lesbian Daughters and FTM Transgender Children*. Toronto: Demeter, 2012.

Pillemer, Karl, and J. Jill Suitor. "Exploring Mothers' Ambivalence toward Their Adult Children." *Journal of Marriage and Family* 64 (2002): 601–13.

ProCon.org. "Gay Marriage Pros and Cons." Accessed June 25, 2014. http://gaymarriage.procon.org/.

Proulx, Christine M., and Heather M. Helms. "Mothers' and Fathers' Perception of Change and Continuity in Their Relationships with Young Adult Sons and Daughters." *Journal of Family Issues* 29, no. 2 (2008): 234–61.

Reeves, Theresa, Sharon G. Horne, Sharon Scales Rostosky, Ellen D. B. Riggle, Linda R. Baggett, and Rebecca A. Aycock. "Family Members' Support for GLBT Issues: The Role of Family Adaptability and Cohesion." *Journal of GLBT Family Studies* 6, no. 1 (2010): 80–97.

Robinson, Peter. *Gay Men's Relationships across the Life Course.* London: Palgrave Macmillan, 2013.

Rosenfeld, Michael. "Couple Longevity in the Era of Same-Sex Marriage in the United States." *Journal of Marriage and Family* 76, no. 5 (October 2014): 905–18.

Rossi, Alice, and Peter Rossi. *Of Human Bonding: Parent-Child Relations across the Life Course.* New York: Aldine de Gruyter, 1990.

Rostosky, Sharon S., Ellen D. B. Riggle, Todd A. Savage, Staci D. Roberts, and Gilbert Singletary. "Interracial Same-Sex Couples' Perceptions of Stress and Coping: An Exploratory Study." *Journal of GLBT Family Studies* 4, no. 3 (2008): 277–99.

Rothblum, Esther D. "Mars to Venus or Earth to Earth? How Do Families of Origin Fit into GLBTQ Lives?" *Journal of GLBT Family Studies* 10, nos. 1–2 (2014): 231–41.

Sarkisian, Natalia, and Naomi Gerstel. "Till Marriage Do Us Part: Adult Children's Relationships with Their Parents." *Journal of Marriage and Family* 70 (2008): 360–76.

Sharp, Elizabeth A., and Lawrence Ganong. "I'm a Loser, I'm Not Married, Let's Just All Look at Me." *Journal of Family Issues* 32, no. 7 (July 2011): 956–80.

Sherman, Mark. "Supreme Court Ruling a Big Win for Gay Marriage." *Worcester (MA) Telegram and Gazette*, October 7, 2014, A9.

Shuey, Kim, and Melissa Hardy. "Assistance to Aging Parents and Parents-in-Law: Does Lineage Affect Family Allocation Decisions?" *Journal of Marriage and Family* 65 (2003): 418–31.

Shulman, Julie L., Gabrielle Gotta, and Robert-Jay Green. "Will Marriage Matter? Effects of Marriage Anticipated by Same-Sex Couples." *Journal of Family Issues* 33, no. 2 (2012): 158–81.

Simmons, T., and M. O'Connell. "Married-Couple and Unmarried-Partner Households: 2000." *Census 2000 Special Reports*, February 2003.

Smith-Acuna, Shelly. *Systems Theory in Action: Applications to Individual, Couple, and Family Therapy.* Hoboken, NJ: Wiley, 2011.

Solomon, Sondra E., Esther D. Rothblum, and Kimberly F. Balsam. "Money, Housework, Sex, and Conflict: Same-Sex Couples in Civil Unions, Those Not in Civil Unions, and Heterosexual Married Siblings." *Sex Roles* 52 (May 2005): 561–75.

Stacey, Judith. "Gay and Lesbian Families: Queer Like Us." In *Family in Transition*, edited by Arlene S. Skolnick and Jerome H. Skolnick, 496–518. Boston: Pearson Allyn & Bacon, 2011.

Stacey, Judith, and Timothy J. Biblarz. "(How) Does the Sexual Orientation of Parents Matter?" *American Sociological Review* 66 (2001): 159–83.

Stone, Leroy O., Carolyn J. Rosenthal, and Ingrid Arnet Connidis. *Parent-Child Exchanges of Support and Intergenerational Equity.* Ottawa, Canada: Statistics Canada, 1998.

Suitor, J. Jill, and Karl Pillemer. "Choosing Daughters: Exploring Why Mothers Favor Adult Daughters over Sons." *Sociological Perspectives* 49, no. 2 (2006): 221–30.

Svab, Alenka, and Roman Kuhar. "The Transparent and Family Closets: Gay Men and Lesbians and Their Families of Origin." *Journal of GLBT Family Studies* 10, no. 1 (2014): 15–35.

Thornton, Arland, Terri L. Orbuch, and William G. Axinn. "Parent-Child Relations during the Transition to Adulthood." *Journal of Family Issues* 16 (1995): 538–64.

Umberson, Debra. "Relationships between Adult Children and Their Parents: Psychological Consequences for Both Generations." *Journal of Marriage and Family* 54 (1992): 664–74.

U.S. Bureau of Labor Statistics. "Marriage and Divorce: Patterns by Gender, Race, and Educational Attainment." *Monthly Labor Review* (October 2013): 1–19.

van Eeden-Moorefield, Brad, Christopher R. Martell, Mark Williams, and Marilyn Preston. "Same-Sex Relationships and Dissolution: The Connection between Heteronormativity and Homonormativity." *Family Relations* 60 (December 2011): 562–71.

Wang, Wendy. "Record Share of Americans Have Never Married." Pew Research Center, Social and Demographic Trends, September 24, 2014. Accessed May 28, 2015. http://www.pewsocialtrends.org/.

Watson, Janet B. "Bisexuality and Family: Narratives of Silence, Solace, and Strength." *Journal of GLBT Family Studies* 10, nos. 1–2 (2014): 101–23.

White, Lynn. "The Effect of Parental Divorce and Remarriage on Parental Support of Adult Children." *Journal of Family Issues* 13, no. 2 (1992): 234–50.

Willson, Andrea E., Kim M. Shuey, and Glenn H. Elder Jr. "Ambivalence in the Relationships of Adult Children to Aging Parents and In-Laws." *Journal of Marriage and Family* 65 (2003): 1055–72.

Index

About the Author

Deborah M. Merrill is professor of sociology at Clark University. Her research focuses on the relationships between parents and adult children as well as on marriage. She has published three other books, book chapters, and articles in this area. Her books include *Caring for Elderly Parents: Juggling Work, Family, and Caregiving in Middle and Working Class Families* (1997), *Mothers-in-Law and Daughters-in-Law: Understanding the Relationship and What Makes Them Friends or Foe* (2007), and *When Your Children Marry: How Marriage Changes Relationships with Sons and Daughters* (2011).